THE ORGANIZATION
OF
PUBLIC EDUCATION
IN SASKATCHEWAN

BY

JAMES D DENNY, B A.

Superintendent of Public Schools
Regina, Sask

A Thesis submitted to the Ontario College of Education in partial fulfilment of the requirements for the Degree of Doctor of Paedagogy.

THE ONTARIO COLLEGE OF EDUCATION
UNIVERSITY OF TORONTO,
1929.

CONTENTS

Contents—*Continued*

Contents—Continued

LIST OF TABLES

THE ORGANIZATION OF PUBLIC EDUCATION IN SASKATCHEWAN

I THE GENESIS OF EDUCATIONAL FACILITIES

As a result of negotiations with the Hudson's Bay Company possession was secured by the Government of Canada of Rupert's land and the adjoining territory extending westward to the Rocky Mountains Out of these lands the province of Manitoba was established in 1870, and the following year the Dominion Parliament passed the North West Territories Act which provided for the government of the remainder of this territory by a council of twelve members with the Lieutenant Governor of Manitoba as president of the council [1] The first legally constituted meeting of this council of the North West Territories was held at Government House, Fort Garry, in March 1873, under the presidency of Lieutenant Governor Morris of Manitoba [2] While the powers of the Council were limited, it passed many ordinances helpful to the maintenance of peace and in the administration of justice in the Territories It also forwarded to the Dominion Government, suggestions and recommendations of great value In relation to education it recommended that schools should be provided for the Indians and that teachers should be furnished to teach them the arts of agriculture This suggestion was adopted with beneficial results [3]

The Council in session in 1874 passed two acts for the protection and education of children [4] The first of these was an Act to regulate the relations existing between religious institutions and children committed to their care The second was intended to regulate the conditions of orphan or destitute children attending schools in the North West Territories These Acts applied to schools or institutions maintained by voluntary contributions The schools were bound to provide proper nutriment, medical care, clothing and education to the child until he reached the age of sixteen years

In 1875 the Dominion Government passed a second North West Territories Act which came into force October 1876 By this Act the government of the Territories was divorced entirely from that of Manitoba and placed under a Lieutenant-Governor of the Territories and a Council not exceeding five members constituted and appointed by the Governor General with the advice of the Queen's Privy Council for Canada [5] The members of the new Council were sworn in on November 27, 1876, at Livingstone, Swan River

The new Act provided for a resident Lieutenant Governor, and the Honorable David Laird, (then Minister of the Interior in the

---

1 *Statutes of Canada, 1871, c 16*, p. 82
2 *History of Saskatchewan*, Dr N F Black, Vol 1, p 123
3 *The Canadian North West*, Dr E H Oliver, p 1001
4 *Ibid*, 1034-1035
5 *Statutes of Canada, 1875, c 45, s 2, 3*

Domin on Parliament) was appointed by the Governor General in
Council to this important position, to hold office during the pleasure
of the Governor General He was required to administer the government of the Territories under instructions given to him from time to
time by Order-in-Council or by the Secretary of State of Canada By
Section 13 of this Act provision was made whereby electoral districts
could be erected by proclamation of the Lieutenant Governor so soon
as any district of the Territories not exceeding in area one thousand
square miles should contain a population of one thousand inhabitants
of adult age, exclusive of aliens or unenfranchised Indians, and should
the population of the district increase to two thousand such inhabit
ants it would be entitled to elect a second representative to the North
West Council When the number of elected members amounted to
twenty one the Council hereinbefore appointed should cease and be
determined, and the members so elected should be constituted and
designated as the Legislative Assembly of the North West Territories
and all the powers by this Act vested in the Council should be henceforth vested in and exercised by the said Legislative Assembly

The Council was entrusted with such powers, not inconsistent
with the Act, as might be from time to time conferred upon it by
the Governor General in Council The Lieutenant Governor by and
with the advice and consent of the Council was empowered to make
provision for the administration of justice and the framing of ordinances in matters of local concern

Clause 11, of the North West Territories Act of 1875 [6] related
to education, and subsequently was the cause of much agitation and
embittered feelings, as it made possible the establishment of separate
schools in the Territories

It read as follows
When, and so soon as any system of taxation shall be adopted in
any district or portion of the North West Territories, the Lieutenant-Governor by and with the consent of the Council or Assembly as the case may be, shall pass all necessary ordinances
in respect to education, but it shall therein be always provided,
that a majority of the ratepayers of any district or portion of
the North West Territories, or any lesser portion or sub-division
thereof, by whatever name the same may be known, may establish such schools therein as they may think fit, and make the
necessary assessment and collection of taxes therefor, and further
that the minority of the ratepayers therein whether Protestant
or Roman Catholic, may establish separate schools therein, and
that, in such latter case, the ratepayers establishing such Protestant or Roman Catholic separate schools shall be liable only
to the assessments of such rates as they may impose upon themselves in respect thereof "

The first legislative session of the Council of the North West
Territories was begun and held at Livingstone, Swan River, on the
eighth day of March 1877, while the Legislative building was in
process of erection at Battleford, the new seat of government The
Honorable David Laird presided as Lieutenant Governor The other
members of this Council were, Matthew Ryan and Lieutenant Colonel

___

6 *Statutes of Canada, 1875, 38 Vict C 49*

Hugh Richardson, Stipendiary Magistrates, and ex-officio Members of Council, and Lieutenant-Colonel Farquharson MacLeod, C M G , Commissioner of the North West Mounted Police, an appointed member, with Amedee E Forget, as Clerk of the Council [7]

At this first session a petition was received from Moise Ouellette and Pierre Landry praying for assistance towards the erection of a school house and the support of a teacher at St Laurent [8] The Council had the question of education thus presented directly to it They considered the petition and passed the following resolution

"Resolved that the Council requests His Honor to reply to the Petitioners and inform them that there are no funds in the hands of the Council applicable to educational purposes, and that the Council do not think it expedient, at present, to consider the question of establishing a system of taxation, and also that His Honor be good enough to express to the Petitioners the regret of the Council that it is unable to grant assistance for so laudable an object as the advancement of Education in the North West "

At the request of the Council the Lieutenant-Governor transmitted a copy of the petition to the Minister of the Interior at Ottawa so that the Dominion Government might be made acquainted with the desire of the people of St Laurent, which desire it believed extended to other settlements in the Territories

Accompanying the petition was the following despatch of the Lieutenant Governor to the Minister of the Interior [9]

"As it does not appear that the Council has now the power to impose direct taxation, except in Electoral Districts, I fear that, without some allowance from the Federal Government for general purposes such as is granted to the Provinces, the children in small settlements in isolated sections of the Territories must grow up in ignorance This is a result to be deplored, as a large portion of the rising generation will thus remain in a great measure unfitted not only to exercise the franchise intelligently when they obtain the privilege, but also the active duties of life "

The reply of January 14, 1878 received from the Minister of the Interior suggested a remedy for the difficulty as follows [10]

"While agreeing with you that the Council of the North West Territories has not power to impose direct taxation for school or other purposes, it appears to me that the Council might obtain the end in view, namely, the raising of a fund for School Corporations and giving them the right to impose a school rate The constitutional objections of want of representation which would apply in the case of taxation by the Council would not be applicable to School Corporations who would merely tax themselves

"In the event of School Corporations being established as above suggested and it is found necessary to supplement the amount raised by them, the amount so required should be

----

7   *Journals of the Council of the North West Territories, 1877,* p 5
8   *Ibid, 1877,* p 10, 24
9   „ *1878,* p 39
10   „ *1878,* p 40

11

placed in your estimates for the Government of the Territories, taking care to indicate the special object for which such amount is required "

The Council acting on this suggestion of the Minister of the Interior included in the estimates for the Government of the North West Territories for the fiscal year, 1879 to 1880, the sum of two thousand dollars in aid of schools. At the same time the Council urged upon the Dominion Government the necessity of amending the North West Territories Act in such a way as to enable the North West Council to pass an ordinance empowering the people of any settlement with a sufficient number of children, to form a school and to assess themselves towards its support [11] The Lieutenant Governor also telegraphed to the Minister of the Interior that he proposed to aid schools supported by missions or voluntary subscriptions to the extent of paying half of the teachers' salaries where there was a minimum average of fifteen scholars in attendance

Prior to the advent of the Canadian Pacific Railway in 1882 there were only a few sparse settlements in widely separate portions of this vast territory The principal of these were at Qu'Appelle, Prince Albert, St Laurent on the south branch of the Saskatchewan, Battleford and Edmonton, with smaller settlements around some of the North West Mounted Police posts, such as MacLeod, Calgary, and Fort Saskatchewan

The Government buildings at Battleford were completed in 1877 and the sessions of the North West Council were held there in 1878, and 1881 [12] But the rapid influx of settlers along the main line of the Canadian Pacific railroad soon necessitated a change in the location of the seat of Government, and resulted in Regina being selected as the capital in 1882

The fifth session of the Council of the North West Territories was held in 1883 It met in Regina, and was presided over by His Honor, 'Edgar Dewdney, who had succeeded the Honorable David Laird as Lieutenant Governor of the Territories in December 1881

While in 1881, only one elected member sat at the Council meetings, namely, Chief Factor Lawrence Clarke of Carleton, member for the District of Lorne, (Prince Albert), in 1883 at the first session held at Regina, six electoral districts were represented, viz Lorne, Edmonton, Broadview, Qu'Appelle, Moose Jaw and Regina The Council was now composed of six elected, [13] five appointed members and the Lieutenant Governor From that time the number of elected members gradually increased until 1888 when the Council was replaced by the Legislative Assembly of the Territories

No session of the Council was convened in 1882 In his address to the Council in 1883, the Lieutenant Governor informed the members that he had but lately received a copy of the Order-in-Council empowering the Lieutenant Governor in Council to make ordinances on the several subjects upon which it was thought most important for them to legislate Accordingly on September 13th, 1883, it was

11   *History of Saskatchewan*, Dr Black, p 198
12   *Ibid*, Dr N F Black p 196
13   *Journals of the Council of North West Territories, 1883*, p 6, 7

agreed that Mr Frank Oliver, member for Edmonton District should have leave to bring in a Bill providing for the organization of public and separate school districts in the North West Territories [14] The Bill was accordingly presented and referred to a special committee of four members to report thereupon. After consideration by the Committee it was laid upon the table

The Bill was printed as reported upon by the committee and distributed to the members of the Council and others interested in education, and many suggestions were received from these gentlemen during the recess of the Council [15]

During the session of Council in 1884, Mr Frank Oliver again introduced his School Bill and on the following day Mr Rouleau presented a second Bill respecting schools in the Territories   The two Bills were referred to the same Special Committee   The Committee considered the two Ordinances and submitted that of Mr. Rouleau to be considered in Committee of the Whole

The first report of the Committee was a recommendation that His Honor be requested to telegraph Ottawa requesting that Section 93 of the British North America Act be put into force in the Territories as provided by Section 9 of the North West Territories Act of 1880,[16] and that the Council proceed with a School Ordinance This being agreed to, the Bill which had been introduced by Mr Rouleau entitled, "An Ordinance Providing for the Organization of Schools in the North West Territories" was amended in Committee of the Whole to render it better adapted to conditions in the Territories, and then on motion of Messrs Rouleau and MacLeod, read a third time and passed [17]

The Standing Committee on Civil Justice later in the session reported, "The Committee have had under consideration the papers relating to the extension of clause 93 of the British North America Act to the Territories and beg leave to recommend that in view of the action of Council on the subject of schools the matter be allowed to stand "[18]

At this time twelve schools with 301 pupils were receiving financial assistance from the Council to the amount of one half of the salaries of the teachers employed, in accordance with the system which had been inaugurated by Lieutenant Governor Laird in December, 1880, at which time he had issued a circular promising financial assistance to schools having an enrolment of fifteen pupils   A strong and unanimous feeling existed among the members of the Council that the Regulations in regard to aid to schools were too stringent, accordingly the following resolution was adopted during the session of 1884

"That the matter of lessening the average attendance, from fifteen as at present required to secure government aid, to ten, be

---

14   *Journals of the Council of the North West Territories, 1883*, p 33
15   *Ibid , 1884*, p 8
16   ,,   *1884*, p 13, 91
17   ,,   *1884*, p 81
18   ,,   *1884*, p 80

referred to the Executive Council in order that the desired
change be brought more directly to the notice of the Government That the Council is of the opinion that the requirements
of the Government should be made as liberal as possible as owing
to the comparatively sparsely settled conditions of the country in
small districts, it is in most instances, impossible to comply with
the present regulations "

This was secured by Ordinance No 3 of 1885, wherein the re-
quirement was placed at "not less than ten, between the ages of
five and sixteen "[19]

After Council rose, it was found that the clauses granting aid to
schools could not be put into operation Notwithstanding this, so
eager were even the earliest settlers to secure the advantages of
education for their children, and such an impetus had been given to
the organization of school districts by the passing of the School Ordinance of 1884 that in a little over twelve months from the date of its
passing no fewer than sixty-five applications for the erection of school
districts had been submitted to the Lieutenant Governor, and thirty-
eight of these had been proclaimed [20]

At the session of the Council in 1885, the Ordinance was so
amended and consolidated that practically a new Ordinance was
passed to take effect early in 1886, in which provision was made for
separate schools as required by Section 14 of the North West Territories Act The schools in the Territories may therefore, be said to
have come under the operation of a School Law on and after the
1st day of April, 1886

By the Ordinance of 1885, the Lieutenant Governor in Council
was empowered to appoint and constitute a Board of Education for
the North West Territories composed of five members, two of whom
would be Roman Catholics and two Protestants, and the Lieutenant
Governor, who would act as Chairman This Board was required to
meet at least twice a year in Regina and was assigned definite powers
for the organization and management of the schools and the carrying
out of the provisions of the School Ordinance [21]

By Clause 6 of this Act the Council was required to resolve itself
into two sections, the one consisting of the Protestant, and the other
of the Roman Catholic members of the Board Each section had
under its control and management the schools designated, Protestant
and Roman Catholic respectively The duties of the Board of
Education were defined as

"(a)   to appoint and remunerate inspectors,

(b)   to appoint a Board of Examiners for the examination of
teachers, and to provide for the expenses of the same,

(c)   to arrange for the examination and certificating of teachers,

(d)   to make regulations for the general organization and administration of all schools,

19   *Journals of the Council of the North West Territories, 1885* p 4
20   *Ibid , 1885* p 7
21   ,,   *1885*, p 39, *and Ordinances of North West Territories*, No 3, *1885*, s 1

14

(*e*) to select, adopt, and prescribe a uniform series of text books to be used in the schools of each section "

In 1887 the following clause was added which defined more definitely the duties of each section of the Board

' Each section of the Board shall have the selection of text books for the examination of teachers in history and science and it shall have the power to prescribe any additionl subjects of examination for the teachers of the schools of its section, and in all examinations on such subjects the examiners of each section shall respectively have exclusive jurisdiction "[22]

In 1887, the School Ordinance was considerably altered in pursuance of the following recommendations of the Board of Education

' Further experience in the working of the School Ordinance and its amendments has disclosed many deficiencies In several school districts difficulties have arisen which necessitated the reference of the disputed clauses for legal advice The Board is advised that many sections of the Ordinance are inoperative and and it has been found that the Board could take no action for the removal of the difficulties spoken of It has also been pointed out that several sections are defective, inasmuch as their provisions are not in accordance with the North West Territories Act "

Accordingly the Protestant members of the Board, who only had an opportunity of considering the matter, prepared a new Ordinance of which they had copies printed for presentation to Council for its consideration at its next session [23]

Owing to the large increase in the number of schools the constitution of the Board of Education was changed in the final session of the North West Council in 1887 to five Protestant and three Roman Catholic members, and the Board appointed one of their number to be Chairman A majority of the Board constituted a quorum [24]

The ninth and final session of the North West Council closed on Saturday, November 19th, 1887

When the Dominion Parliament met early in 1888 the North West Territories Act was amended abolishing the Council and creating a Legislative Assembly of twenty-five members, twenty-two of whom were to be elected and three appointed from the judiciary of the Territories as legal experts [25] The latter acted in an advisory capacity and had the like privileges as the elected members except that they were not entitled to vote The members were elected for three years Provision was also made for a committee of four members who with the Lieutenant Governor would constitute an Advisory Council in all matters of finance [26] The Lieutenant Governor was Chairman of this council and had the right to vote as a member thereof and also had a casting vote in case of a tie

---

22   *Ordinances of North West Territories 1887, No 2, s 10,* p 60
23   *Report of the Board of Education, 1886-1887,* p 15
24   *Ordinances of the North West Territories, 1887, No 2, s 1*
25   *Statutes of Canada 1888, 51, Victoria, c 19,*
26   *Ibid , c 19, s 13*

II THE DEVELOPMENT OF LEGISLATIVE CONTROL

A CONSTITUTIONAL QUESTION

1889-1892

The Legislative Assembly was now an elective body of the people, and the members wishing to make it responsible as well, claimed the right of control of the moneys voted by the Dominion Parliament for the expenditures of the North West Government, either directly or through a council or committee The North West Territories Act did not clearly provide for such a system The clause in the Act relating thereto read as follows

> "The Lieutenant Governor shall select from among the elected members of the Legislative Assembly, four persons to act as an Advisory Council on matters of finance, who shall severally hold office during pleasure, and the Lieutenant Governor shall preside at all sittings of such Advisory Council and have a right to vote as a member thereof, and shall also have a casting vote in case of a tie."[1]

Lieutenant Governor Royal held that the law required him to expend the Dominion subsidies under the direction of the Dominion Government and not under the advice of the Legislative Assembly As these moneys voted by the Dominion Parliament were apportioned in part for the support of education, this constitutional struggle had an important influence on the progress of educational affairs in the Territories

We find the Assembly maintaining that the powers of legislation and financial control should go together and objecting to being denied the right of control of these "Dominion Funds" At the Session of 1888, the Assembly believing it possessed control of the grant in aid of schools, provided that a certain proportion of aid from that grant should be extended to school districts On the strength of the inducement thus held out, many new districts were organized, taxation was levied and liabilities were incurred for the erection of schoolhouses, whose usefulness depended on the receipt of the proportion of the aid promised in the Ordinance of the Assembly

During the Session of 1889, the promise of the grant remained without any intimation from His Honor that it would not be made good, and a still further increase in the number of school districts took place In the same year, after the annual taxation rate had been struck on the basis of the grant promised by the Assembly, a circular authorized by the Lieutenant Governor was received by the several school districts warning them of a proposed reduction to be made in the amount of their grant On learning of this the Assembly voiced its disapproval in the following resolution

---

1 *Statutes of Canada, 1875, 38 Vict. c. 49*

16

"This House is compelled to inform your Honor that if it
is to understand that the control of the school funds rests with
your Honor and not with the Assembly, as would appear from
the circular referred to, it will be necessary for us to amend
the present Ordinance by striking out the provisions relating
to aid to schools and thereby make known that upon your Honor
rests the responsibility of the distribution of the said fund and
the support of the school system of the North West Territories"

The Assembly again reiterated its position in the following extract from the address in reply to Lieutenant Governor Royal,
November 9th, 1890 [2]

"This Assembly must protest against its being placed in the
position of being responsible to the people of the North West
Territories for proper legislation regarding schools, and yet be
deprived of the control of the funds whereby alone that legislation can be given effect, whereby alone the school system at
present existing in the North West Territories can be maintained"

In the speech from the Throne at the close of the same session,
the Lieutenant Governor re-affirmed his position, refusing to accede
to the Assembly's claim to control the expenditure of the moneys
voted by the Parliament of Canada for the Government of the North
West Territories His Honor made this definite statement to the
Assembly [3]

"While I cannot accede to your claim to control the expenditure of the moneys voted by the Parliament of Canada for
the government of the North-West Territories, I have always
assumed without question the direct control of the expenditure
of the moneys annually voted by the Parliament of Canada for
school purposes in the Territories"

He was upheld in this position by the Dominion Government as
is evidenced by the report of the Minister of Justice of September
29th, 1892, to his Excellency, the Governor General of Canada in
which the Minister states:

"The Parliament of Canada has vested the Executive
Government of the Territories in the Lieutenant Governor, acting under instructions from your Excellency-in-Council, or from
the Secretary of State, with an Advisory Council on matters of
finance (under section 13 of Chapter 19, 1888) or a Committee
(under Chapter 22 of 1891,) composed of members of the Legislative Assembly"

However after much controversy and prolonged negotiations with
the Federal Authorities, a measure of success was attained, and
the right of the Assembly to the control of the finances of the Territories was admitted The Lieutenant Governor was instructed to
account to the Assembly for the expenditure of the Dominion subsidy in a manner similar to that for the other revenues of the Territories

---

2   *Journals of the Legislative Assembly North West Territories, 1890*, p 40.
3   *Ibid*, p 21

The growth in power of the Assembly is very succinctly stated
by Lieutenant Governor Royal in his last speech from the Throne,
September 16th, 1893, as follows

"When on the 4th of July, 1888, I was sworn in as Lieutenant Governor of the North West Territories, I was responsible
to the Privy Council of Canada alone for all executive acts done
in the Territories The Assembly had hardly a voice in the
government of the country, and the Lieutenant Governor was
practically a political commissioner under whose direct supervision and authority the affairs of the Territories were conducted
and administered Now all this has been materially changed
The Legislature to-day practically enjoys the rights and privileges of self-government "[4]

4   *Journals of the Legislative Assembly, North West Territories, 1893,* p 109

III CHANGES IN ADMINISTRATION.

By Ordinance No 22, assented to December 31st, 1892, the old Board of Education was replaced by a Council of Public Instruction. Section 5 of this Ordinance reads as follows [1]

"The members of the Executive Committee of the Territories and four persons, two of whom shall be Protestants, and two Roman Catholics, appointed by the Lieutenant Governor-in-Council shall constitute a Council of Public Instruction, and one of the said Executive Committee, to be nominated by the Lieutenant Governor in Council, shall be Chairman of the said Council of Public Instruction The appointed members shall have no vote The Executive Committee, or any sub-committee thereof appointed for that purpose shall constitute a quorum of the Council of Public Instruction, but no general regulations respecting (a) the management and discipline of schools, (b) the examination, grading and licensing of teachers, (c) the selection of books, (d) the inspection of schools, (e) normal training of teachers, shall be adopted or amended except at a general meeting of the Council of Public Instruction duly convened for that purpose "

Thus the Council was in complete control of all the schools of the Territories There was no longer any division of authority and uniformity in administration was secured The Council was requested to report annually to the Lieutenant Governor upon all the schools, with such statements and suggestions for promoting education as they deemed useful and expedient [2] Section 6 of the same Ordinance also provided that "It shall be lawful for the Lieutenant Governor-in-Council to appoint a Superintendent of Education for the Territories, who shall also be Secretary of the Council of Public Instruction " This was accordingly done in 1893 Dr D J Goggin, formerly Principal of the Manitoba Normal School became the first Superintendent of Education, as well as Principal of the new Normal School for the Territories, situated in Regina, which position he held until the time of his resignation in 1902

By Section 106 of the same Ordinance, it was required that, "all schools shall be taught in the English language, but it shall be permissible for the trustees of any school to cause a primary course to be taught in the French language "[3]

The next important change in the administration of the school system of the Territories came into effect September 1st, 1901, when legislation became effective by which the Council of Public Instruc-

---

1 *Report of Council of Public Instruction, 1896*, p 8
2 *Ordinances of the North West Territories, 1895-1896*, p 12.
3 *Ibid , 1895-1896*, p 12

tion ceased to exist and the control of all matters pertaining to education was entrusted to a newly organized department of the public service of the Territories called the "Department of Education", over which the member of the Executive Council appointed by the Lieutenant Governor-in-Council should preside and discharge the functions of "Commissioner of Education" for the Territories [4]

Mr F W G Haultain, (afterwards, Sir Frederick) who had been Chairman of the Council of Public Instruction, became the first Commissioner of Education and assumed the administration of the department and the control of the educational system.

The Ordinance of 1901, provided also for an "Educational Council"[5] consisting of five persons to be appointed by the Lieutenant Governor-in-Council of whom at least two should be Roman Catholics

All general regulations respecting the inspection of schools, the training and licensing of teachers, course of study, text and reference books, etc , were required to be referred to the Council for consideration, and for report thereon before being adopted or amended   The Council also considered any questions referred to it by the Commissioner and had the right to consider and report to the Lieutenant Governor-in-Council on any question concerning the educational system of the Territories [6]

The Educational Council held its first meeting July 31st, 1902, and considered various questions submitted to it by the "Department"   Of these the most important was the revision of the regulations governing teachers' certificates, and the revision of the course of study for the High School standards   In the latter revision the principle of elective studies was first introduced

---

5   *Ordinances of the North West Territories, 1901, c 29, s 3*
4   *Ibid , 1901, c 29, s 8*
6   *,, 1901, c 29, s 10, 11*

IV   THE ESTABLISHMENT OF PROVINCIAL CONTROL

The agitation in the North West Territories for full provincial
autonomy, a position to which the Territories had been advancing
gradually, was realized in the passing of the Alberta and Saskatchewan Acts in 1905   The Saskatchewan Act which came into force
on the first day of September, 1905, was an Act to establish and
provide for the government of the new Province of Saskatchewan
which had been established from part of the Territories

Provision was made in this Act for the establishment of a system of separate schools in the new province, it being claimed that the
clause in the British North America Act protecting the separate
school system should be extended to the new province   By Section
(3) of the Saskatchewan Act of 1905, the provisions of The British
North America Acts, 1867 to 1886, were applied to the Province of
Saskatchewan in the same way and to the like extent as they apply
to the provinces heretofore comprised in the Dominion, as if, the
said province of Saskatchewan had been one of the provinces origin-
ally united, except in so far as varied by this Act, and except such
provisions as are in terms made, or by reasonable intendment may be
held to be, specially applicable to or only to affect one or more and
not the whole of the said provinces

Section 93 of the British North America Act relates to education
and reads as follows [1]

"In and for each province the legislature may exclusively
make laws in relation to education, subject and according to the
following provisions

"(*1*) Nothing in any such law shall prejudicially affect any
right or privilege with respect to denominational schools which
any class of persons have by law in the province at the Union

"(*3*) Where in any province a system of separate or dis-
sentient schools exists by law at the Union, or is thereafter
established by the Legislature of the Province, an appeal shall
lie to the Governor General in Council from any Act or decision
of any Provincial authority affecting any right or privilege of
the Protestant or Roman Catholic minority of the Queen's
subjects in relation to education "

Clause 17 of the Saskatchewan Act relates to education and on
reading it we find that subsection 1 of section 93, of the British
North America Act has been modified   According to clause 17,
section 93 of the British North America Act, 1867, shall apply to the
said Province with the substitution for subsection 1 of the said section
93, of the following paragraphs

"(*1*) Nothing in any such law shall prejudicially affect any

---

1   *W H P Clement, The Canadian Constitution, c 38* p 777

right or privileges with respect to separate schools which any
class of persons have at the date of the passing of this Act, under
the terms of Chapters 29 and 30 of the Ordinance of the North
West Territories, passed in the year 1901, or with respect to
religious instruction in any public or separate school as provided
for in said ordinances "

"(2) In the appropriation by the Legislature or distribution
by the Government of the Province of any moneys for the support
of schools organized and carried on in accordance with the said
chapter 29, or any Act passed in amendment thereof, or in substitution therefor, there shall be no discrimination against schools
of any class described in the said chapter 29 "

"(3) Where the expression "by law" is employed in paragraph 3 of the said section 93, it shall be held to mean the law
as set out in the said chapters 29 and 30, and where the expression "At the Union" is employed, in the said paragraph 3, it
shall be held to mean the date at which this Act comes into
force."

This clause made it quite evident that separate schools with all
the rights and religious privileges enjoyed under the ordinances of the
North West Territories of 1901 were to be perpetuated These ordinances provided that the minority of the ratepayers in any district
whether Protestant or Roman Catholic might establish a separate
school and be exempted from school assessment except for that
separate school

When the Province of Saskatchewan was organized in 1905 the
School Ordinances which had so successfully met the requirements of
the North West Territories were continued in force without change
during the year 1906 The Deputy Commissioner in his report for
1906 makes the following statement relative thereto

"These Ordinances have satisfactorily stood the test of
several years and it cannot be gainsaid that they have met well
the requirements of a new country This being so, there seemed
no pressing necessity of interfering with a school system which
was intended not only to keep up the standing of schools and
the professional qualifications of teachers, but also to grant every
assistance to districts struggling with the difficulties incident to
a new country."[2]

The Department of Education which had existed since 1901 as
a distinct and separate branch of the public service presided over by
the Commissioner of Education, who was one of the members of the
Executive Council, continued as the executive or administrative body
in educational affairs The Educational Council also continued to
function but as some of its members lived in the newly formed province of Alberta, it became necessary to constitute a new Council for
the Province of Saskatchewan, which was done by Order-in-Council
in June 1906 Its duties continued to be those in accordance with
the provisions of the School Ordinance in that behalf

---

2   *Report of Department of Education, 1906, p 7*

Provision for the establishment of separate schools in Saskatchewan (then part of the North West Territories) was made under clause 11 of the North West Territories Act of 1875 But it was not until the establishment of the Public School system in 1884 that the first separate schools were erected At that time schools were organized at Regina, Moose Jaw, Qu'Appelle and Prince Albert At the present time, December 31, 1927, 4776 school districts have been established, in only 31 of which there are separate schools In 23 of these the separate school is Roman Catholic, while the other eight are Protestant separate schools [3] The separate schools are under the same regulations as the public schools as to course of study, teachers' certificates, professional training of teachers, etc and are inspected by the same government inspectors, so that they are as directly under the control of the Department of Education as are the public schools The same standards of educational attainment are demanded from both the pupils and teachers of the separate schools as from those of the public schools The Grade VIII pupils of both classes of schools are required to pass the same examinations for admission to the High Schools, while all students in secondary schools are subject to the same examinations for teachers' certificates, and all teachers qualifying for the same grade of certificate must take the same professional training

Although separate schools might be established within the boundaries of any district by a Protestant or Roman Catholic minority, relatively little advantage has been taken of this provision, as such schools receive no special privileges other than the segregation of the pupils of the same faith

---

[3] *Annual Report, Department of Education, 1927,* p 37
See Table X V p 195

V   SOCIAL CONDITIONS IN SASKATCHEWAN

One of the most serious educational problems in the early days of the province arose from the rapid influx of people of many foreign nationalities and the settlement of many of them according to the block or "colony" system   There were many districts settled solely by colonies of Swedes, Finns, Germans, Russians, Hungarians, Bohemians, Austrians, Galicians, Poles, Icelanders, Mennonites, Doukhobors and others

This rapid increase of a foreign and relatively illiterate population was at once a challenge and an invitation to the educational institutions and authorities of the province   The necessity of assimilating these different races and of securing their co-operation in the building up of a new country was a problem demanding tact, patience, and tolerant but definite legislation

It could hardly be expected that the older members of these races lately arrived from Europe where they had been trained, in different social customs, under different political institutions, and nurtured in thoughts and ideals foreign to those of Canadians, would readily renounce the ideals to which they and their ancestors had been accustomed for centuries, for those of this new land   Consequently it is largely through the education of the younger generation that it has become possible to train gradually these different races to learn our social system, to acquire some sense of civic responsibility and to understand and appreciate the benefits of the laws and institutions of the country of their adoption

The block plan of settlement retarded assimilation   It was difficult to get Canadian teachers to accept positions as teachers in these foreign districts because of the lack of congenial society and of comfortable places in which to live   Where this was possible the progress made was most encouraging   The best work was found to be accomplished by English-speaking teachers unacquainted with the language of the people of the school district

The Galicians and Doukhobors were, generally speaking, poor and illiterate, and quite ignorant of the value of an education for their children   Frequently they looked upon the schools with suspicion and were violently hostile to the creation of a school district and to the direct tax for school purposes, and had little or no desire to have their children learn English   In some cases this hostility and the absence of schools in their settlements may be traced to the fact that these people had been accustomed to having things done for them and consequently hesitated to take the initial steps required by law for organizing a district   The Government recognizing this fact appointed a supervisor of schools who in 1908 organized thirty-one school districts in Ruthenian and Doukhobor settlements

He recommended to the Department that for the benefit of the foreign population legislation should be provided to ensure the following

> (a) compulsory organization of school districts,
>
> (b) management of these schools by an official trustee,
>
> (c) compulsory education to enforce regularity of attendance at school

Irregularity of attendance was a prevailing characteristic in many of the schools in the foreign settlements One school inspector reports in 1913 as follows "I visited one school where the enrolment was 33 Only 4 pupils were present, and 20 of the 33 were under ten years of age During the fall I visited in succession 18 schools where the total enrolment was 469 Only 129 pupils were present at the time of my visits or about 25 per cent of the enrolment The majority of these schools were in Ruthenian or German districts "

The majority of the old orthodox Mennonites came to Canada from Southern Russia Many of these settled in colonies or village communities and opposed the formation of public school districts within their settlements They believed that through learning the English language their children would tend to leave the colony Consequently they organized parochial private schools taught in the German language with the Bible and catechism as the chief reading texts, and the parents were forbidden by the autocratic leaders of the colony or community to send their children to the public schools The children were denied their birth-right as Canadians More hopeful conditions existed in districts or communities settled by people of several nationalities including English-speaking In such districts English became the language of communication The children attended the same school in, which only English was taught, and in which the ideals of Canadian citizenship were inculcated by a sympathetic and thoroughly qualified Canadian teacher

The Poles, Slovaks and Bohemians were as a whole fairly interested in education and desired their children to secure a good working knowledge of the English language These people and their children adapted themselves more readily to Canadian conditions

Immigrants from the Scandinavian countries are energetic, ambitious and easily adopt Canadian customs They are a sociable people who intermingle freely with the English-speaking families and are thus easily assimilated into a high type of Canadian citizenship

The greatest hope for the Canadianization of this ever-increasing cosmopolitan population, and the greatest factor in the process of assimilation is the public school, particularly those schools in which children of several races intermingle in class and in play, with English as the common medium of communication On the other hand the colony system of settlement with its accompanying parochial school and spirit of separatism, and a minimum teaching of English, is detrimental to a training in Anglo-Saxon ideals and the fundamental principles of true Canadian citizenship

The legislators of the province cognizant of the great task and their stupendous duty of raising the social status of these peoples and of training them to an appreciation and adoption of Canadian ideals and customs, have gradually and tolerantly, but persistently enforced regulations by which the common school is fast becoming the paramount influence in this great work of creating in these people both the will and the capacity to fulfil their duties in a representative constitution

"The struggle for the elimination of illiteracy in the Prairie Provinces in the five years, 1921-1926, is most interesting On the whole illiteracy decreased very considerably during the five years, which indicates that the schools have been very effective This is emphasized by the fact that decreases were especially strong between the ages of 10 and 20 years Analysis shows, however, that except at the ages of 10 to 20 the decreases were largely confined to the Canadian and British born Even at the ages mentioned there were cases of foreign born showing increased illiteracy In nearly all cases the ages 65 and over showed absolute increases What seemed to be of special importance, however, is that in the case of the foreign born (in practically all cases the Canadian and British improved) the rural areas showed decided improvement, except at the age of 65 and over, but the urban areas showed very little improvement, and in many cases gave indications of reaction This applies especially to absolute figures, but also in some cases to percentages illiterate It also applies to females to a greater extent than to males There are strong indications of a movement of aged, and also younger adult illiterate foreign females from rural to urban areas "[1]

TABLE I ILLITERACY OF POPULATION, 10 YEARS AND OVER, 1926

23 754 persons or   3 99% of the population are illiterate
4,114 persons or   1 33% of the Canadian-born are illiterate
19,434 persons or 10 18% of the Foreign-born are illiterate
206 persons or a very insignificant number of British-born
(less than one-fourth of one per cent) are illiterate [2]

The cosmopolitan nature of the population of the province may be more definitely appreciated from the following statement of the percentages of the population represented by the different nationalities, and also by the birth places of the population as tabulated below

TABLE II   RACIAL COMPOSITION OF THE POPULATION IN
1926 [3]

Total   population—820,738,   males—446,536,   females—374,202

British	50 77 per cent	Russians	4 41 per cent
Ukranian	6 27 per cent	Austrian	2 41 per cent
French	5 73 per cent	Hungarians	1 50 per cent
Dutch	2 53 per cent	Poles	1 75 per cent
German	11 76 per cent	Indians	1 58 per cent
Scandinavian	7 72 per cent	All others	4 57 per cent
including Icelandic			

---

1   *Annual Survey of Education in Canada, 1927 Cap 1*, p XIV
2   *Census of Saskatchewan, 1926*, p 178
3   *Ibid , 1926* p 81

26

TABLE III   BIRTH-PLACE OF TOTAL POPULATION,
1926 [4]

Canada	63 45 per cent
British Isles	12 14 per cent
Other British Possessions	13 per cent
Europe	14 52 per cent
Asia	39 per cent
United States	9 33 per cent
Others	04 per cent

TABLE IV   URBAN AND RURAL POPULATION
1901 to 1926

by Quinquennial Periods

Census Year	Urban[1]	Rural	Total	Per cent of Population		Increase per cent over Preceding Census	
				Urban	Rural	Urban	Rural
1901	14,266	77,013	91,279	15 63	84 37		
1906	48,462	209,301	257,763	18.80	81 20	239 70	171 77
1911	131,395	361,037	492,432	26 68	73 32	171 13	72 50
1916	176,162	471,673	647,835	27 21	72 79	34 17	30 61
1921	218 958	538,552	757,510	28 90	71 10	24 20	14 21
1926	242,532	578,206	820,738	29 55	70 45	10 77	7 36

1   *Urban includes people living in incorporated villages, towns, and cities*

4   *Census of Sask , 1926*, p 81

VI MUNICIPAL GOVERNMENT

When the province of Saskatchewan was established on September 1st, 1905, the local government in that area of the North West Territories, which now comprises the Province of Saskatchewan, consisted of the two rural municipalities of Indian Head and South Qu'Appelle, a considerable number of local improvement districts with very limited powers, and a few towns and villages

In the year 1906 the Provincial Government appointed a special Municipal Commission to inquire into and recommend a suitable system of municipal institutions for the province This committee reported in the year 1907, and in the years 1908 and 1909 the Legislature passed the City, Town, Village and Rural Municipality Acts thereby instituting the system of municipal government under which, with future amendments, the municipalities are governed at present. The Legislature, at the same time, passed the Municipal Affairs Act creating a Department of the government in charge of a Minister of the Crown, to exercise a general supervision over the municipalities brought into existence under this system [1] This department came into existence on November 1st, 1908

At the time of the establishment of the Department of Municipal Affairs the municipal institutions of the province consisted of 4 cities, 43 towns, 108 villages, 2 rural municipalities, and 359 local improvement districts Outside of the rural municipalities of Indian Head and South Qu'Appelle these local improvement districts were the only form of rural municipal organization then in existence in the province

On December 13, 1909, these small districts were disorganized and the province divided according to a general plan into "territorial units" of nine townships or an area of 324 square miles each [2] That portion of the province which had been previously organized into small local improvement districts, along with several additional townships, was erected into larger local improvement districts each comprising the area of a territorial unit Provision was made for the gradual erection of these areas into rural municipalities with full municipal powers and responsibilities By the end of the year 1912 the number of rural municipalities in the province had increased to 200, while the number of local improvement districts had been reduced to 90

By special legislation passed at the end of the year 1912 all local improvement districts were declared to be rural municipalities on and after January 1st, 1913 [3] The number of rural municipalities

---

1   *Revised Statutes of Sask , 1920, chap 19 Vol 1*
2   *Statutes of Sask , 1908, c 7, s 3*
3   *Ibid , 1912-13, c 30, s 4*

has continued to increase until at the end of 1927 there were 301 in the province During the period since 1908 a large number of urban municipalities have also been established, there being at the present time 8 cities, 80 towns, and 377 villages

In rural municipalities the administration is vested in a council composed of a reeve and six councillors Each councillor is elected by the electors of a division of the municipality [4] An elector is a person whose name appears on the last revised voters' list and includes the husbands and wives of persons assessed and residing with such persons on land in the municipality

Generally speaking the assessment for purposes of taxation in rural municipalities is limited to the land Under the statue all land in a rural municipality is assessable at its fair actual value No farmer in Saskatchewan is required to pay taxes on his buildings, stock, implements, or other personal property which he may own.[5] Merchants in a rural municipality are, however, subject to assessment and taxation in respect to their businesses on the basis of a rate of assessment per square foot of the area used in the business Buildings situated in hamlets or unorganized villages are also assessed at 60 per cent of their fair actual value [6]

When a hamlet attains a population of 100, provision is made for its erection into a village The affairs of the village are administered by a council board of three, elected by the electors [7] As in the case of a rural municipality an elector is a person whose name appears on the last revised voters' list of the village One of the councillors is appointed as overseer of the village at the first meeting of the council Taxes are assessed and levied on lands, buildings, business, and income Land is assessed at its fair actual value and buildings and improvements thereon at sixty per cent of their value Businesses are assessed on a floor space basis, the assessor fixing the rate per square foot of space (irrespective of partitions, elevators, stairways or other obstructions) of each building or part thereof used for business purposes [8] Income is subject to certain statutory exemptions corresponding somewhat to the exemptions allowed under the Dominion Income Tax Law

When the population of a village has increased to 500 persons actually resident therein provision is made for its erection into a town [9] The governing body of a town consists of a mayor and six councillors When a town has attained a population of 5,000 it may be erected into a city [10] In the city the council consists of a mayor and not less than 6 and not more than 20 aldermen, as may be determined by law If a city is divided into wards the number of alder-

---

4   *Rural Municipalities Act, s 21*
5   *Ibid, s. 244, 245 s s 9*
6   *Ibid, s 249, 250*
7   *Village Act, s 8, 29, 35*
8   *Ibid, s 243, 247*
9   *Ibid, s 305-309*
10   *The Town Act, s 574*

men may not exceed four for each ward [11]   The City Council has power to appoint one or more commissioners and place them in charge of certain departments of the city's work   These commissioners are chosen because of their scientific or technical knowledge of certain branches of civic business   In towns and cities land is assessed at its fair actual value, and buildings and improvements thereon at not more than sixty per cent of their value   Business is assessed in the same way as it is in villages, while income is subject to similar statutory exemptions [12]

Thus we find that in cities and towns the sources of municipal taxation are (*1*) lands (including buildings), (*2*) businesses, (*3*) income, and (*4*) special franchises   In villages taxes are levied on the first three while in rural municipalities the great source of municipal taxation is land only   In hamlets or unorganized villages, taxes are also levied by the rural municipality on buildings and business   There is no municipal income tax in a rural municipality   In all municipalities the sources of taxation are the same for municipal and school purposes   Assessment of the property, business, and income subject to taxation is made by the assessor, and after the assessment has been confirmed or amended by the court of revision, and in the case of appeal from the decision of the court by the Saskatchewan Assessment Commission, the taxes for both municipal and school purposes are raised by a levy upon the assessment   In the cases of school taxes the board of trustees of the school district requisitions the council for such amount as will meet the requirements of the district for the year [13]   The council then makes a levy at such rate upon the dollar of the assessment as will produce the required amount   In cities and towns the council is required to collect the school taxes along with the municipal taxes and to pay over same to the board of trustees as received   In villages and rural municipalities the school taxes are a direct liability upon the municipality and the council is required to pay over to the board of trustees the amount of the requisition of the board for the year, in quarterly instalments on March 31, June 30, September 30, and December 31, whether the taxes are collected or not [14]   To enable the councils of villages and rural municipalities to make these payments, the council is empowered to borrow on the credit of the school districts, taxes to an amount not exceeding eighty per cent of the estimated total of the taxes to be collected for the school district in the current year [15]   In cities and towns the board of trustees of the school district has authority to borrow from the bank to meet the current expenditures of the district until the taxes are received from the municipality   We have nothing in this Province to correspond to the township grants of Ontario   In other words the municipalities of Saskatchewan are not required by law to make grants to the school districts situate therein

The only step which has been taken to equalise municipal taxation as between one municipality and another was the establish-

---

11   *The City Act*, s 13, 14
12   *Ibid*, s 432-437
13   *School Assessment Act*, s 34, 35
14   *The Rural Municipalities Act*, s 301, 302
15   *Ibid*, s 221

ment in 1922 of the Saskatchewan Assessment Commission which has done some important work in this regard The Commission is a branch of the Department of Municipal Affairs and is composed of three members appointed by the Lieutenant Governor-in-Council The jurisdiction and powers of the Commission are set out as follows [16]

(a) exercise general supervision over the administration of the assessment provisions of the municipal Acts of the province and over all assessors to the end that assessments shall be made relatively fair and just, and in strict accordance with the requirements of the various municipal Acts,

(b) - confer with, advise and direct assessors, as to their duties,

(c) prescribe a uniform system of procedure to be observed in the preparation of assessment rolls,

(d) require assessors and other municipal officials to make such returns to the commission on any matters affecting the subject of assessment and taxation, and in such forms, as it may from time to time call for,

(e) make rules, not inconsistent with the provisions of this Act, for its own government and for the performance of the duties of assessors, and for conducting hearings and proceedings before it;

(f) summon witnesses to appear and give evidence, and to produce books, papers and documents,

(g) hear assessment appeals under the provisions of the Town Act, The Village Act and The Rural Municipality Act respectively,

(h) perform such other duties as may be designated by any Act of the Legislature or by the Minister "

Provision is also made in The School Assessment Act for an annual adjustment of the proper proportionate amounts to be levied by the municipalities on behalf of the school district where a village or town school district is situated partly in two or more municipalities [17] The Act provides that the assessors of the municipalities concerned shall form an adjustment board and the said board shall meet each year and determine what proportion of the taxes to be levied on behalf of the school district shall be levied upon and collected from the taxable property of the ratepayers of the school district situated in each of the municipalities Where the members of the adjustment board disagree the matter is referred to the Saskatchewan Assessment Commission, which then hears and determines the matter The decision of the Commission is final Similar provision is also made in the Rural Municipality Act for an adjustment of the school taxes to be levied upon the different portions of a school district where such district is situated partly in one rural munici-

---

16 *The Saskatchewan Assessment Commission Act, 1922,* sec 14
17 *School Assessment Act,* s 44-51

pality and partly in another, or partly in a hamlet and partly in a
rural municipality.[18]

While the Elementary schools of the Province have two sources
of financial support

(a) rates levied upon taxable property within the district,

(b) government grants paid in accordance with the provisions of
the School Grants Act,

two rural school districts in which the schools are kept open at least
185 days in the year receive the same assistance from the Government by way of provincial grants, consequently the poorer district
with a much lower total assessment is compelled to carry a much
heavier burden of local taxation to meet similar demands for educational services. As there is no province-wide scheme for the equaliza-
tion of assessments, the burden of supporting or maintaining the schools
in the province is not equally distributed among the municipalities,
consequently the children of the province have not that equality of
opportunity which should characterize a democratic state.

Where a municipality desires to make permanent improvements
it may raise money by the issue of debentures.[19] Authority to issue
such debentures must, however, be obtained from the Local Government Board, an independent commission, whose duty it is to to investigate all applications for authority to borrow money by way of debenture, and to approve or reject the same.[20] (See page 64 for powers
of Local Government Board.)

---

18   *The Rural Municipalities Act*, s. 312-315
19   *The City Act*, s. 329-354
20   *The Revised Statutes of Sask.*, *1920*, c. 23

VII ORGANIZATION OF SCHOOL DISTRICTS

In 1883 the requirements for the establishment of a district were
that.

(*a*) it should not exceed in area thirty-six square miles,

(*b*) the petition for its organization should contain the sig-
natures of at least two-thirds of the electors resident within the
limits of the proposed district,

(*c*) a counter-petition must be signed by at least five electors of the proposed district and presented within the space of
nine weeks from the first insertion by the Lieutenant Governor
of the notice in a local newspaper setting forth the limits, etc ,
of the proposed new district,

(*d*) a vote might be taken to decide whether the district
should be made a School District or not by any number of
resident ratepayers placing in the hands of the Lieutenant Governor the sum of fifty dollars to cover the expense of taking a vote
The wish of a majority of the legally qualified voters as expres-
sed at the poll should prevail

When established, three duly elected trustees exercised the
powers of such district

The Board of Trustees at its first meeting was required to appoint one of its members, Secretary of the Board   It also appointed
one of its members or a responsible resident of the district to be
treasurer

MODIFICATIONS OF THE INITIAL REQUIREMENTS
FOR ORGANIZATION

In 1885, any three resident electors of any area of not more than
thirty-six square miles, its extreme limits being not more than nine
miles apart, might form themselves into a committee to procure the
erection of a school district and might petition the Lieutenant Governor for such erection   Public or Separate school districts might be
erected if there were not less than four resident heads of families and
ten children between the ages of five and sixteen in the proposed
district

On receiving the report of a first school meeting the Lieutenant
Governor was authorized, if the majority of the votes at the school
district meeting had been in favor of the erection of the school district, to forthwith proclaim the area a school district in accordance
with the terms of the petition addressed to him in that behalf [1]

---

1   *Ordinances of the North-West Territories, 1885,* no 3

In 1888 this was changed to read,[2]

"Any three ratepayers, two of whom shall be heads of families resident in any district comprising an area of not more than twenty-five square miles if there are four resident families and ten children of school age, which shall mean between the ages of five and twenty inclusive."

In 1895 it was again modified to any three ratepayers, with no proviso

In 1896, a school district was required to comprise an area of not more than twenty-five square miles, which should not be more than five miles in breadth or length exlusive of road allowances, and should contain not less than four resident ratepayers and twelve children between the ages of five and sixteen years inclusive, except in special cases wherein the chairman of the council might permit an enlargement of the above mentioned boundaries if all the resident ratepayers affected agreed in writing to the same [3] These conditions were later modified to read twenty square miles and ten children

If the above conditions were fulfilled any three resident ratepayers might petition the chairman of the Council of Public Instruction for the erection of a school district and on receiving its consent could proceed with the organization of the district The committees entrusted with the initial steps of organization generally felt that districts embracing an area varying from sixteen to twenty square miles were sufficiently large to be easily accessible to children who had to attend the school from the outlying portions of the district

In accordance with the provisions of the North West Territories Act providing for the establishment of separate schools it was lawful for any number of the ratepayers whether Protestant or Roman Catholic, the same being a minority of the ratepayers resident within the limits of an organized public school district, to establish a separate school therein, by proclamation of the Lieutenant Governor, with the same rights, powers, privileges, liabilities, and method of government as was provided in the ordinances for public school districts. The petition for such separate school district was required to be signed by three ratepayers, two of whom were resident heads of families of the religious faith indicated in the name of the proposed district When such Protestant or Roman Catholic separate school was erected, all property comprised in such district belonging to or held by ratepayers of the religious faith indicated by the name of such district was liable only to such assessments as they might impose upon themselves in respect thereof [4]

Within ten months after the issue of the Order in Council erecting a newly organized district the trustees were required to engage a qualified person as school teacher for such period not exceeding one year and at such salary as might be agreed upon [5] All schools were

2 *School Ordinances, 1885*, s 18, 19, p 433
3 *Ordinances of the North-West Territories, 1896*, sec 12
4 *Ibid , 1888*, s 37-41
5 *Ibid, No 2, 1896*, s 96

to be taught in the English language but it was permissible for the
trustees of any school to cause a primary course to be taught in the
French language [6] By section 114 permission was granted to any
school in the Territories to establish Kindergarten classes for the
teaching and training of children between the ages of four and six
years according to Kindergarten methods Permission was also
granted to the trustees of any school district to engage a qualified
teacher and make the necessary arrangements at the expense of the
school district for the maintenance of a night school It was permissible to charge a stated fee for attendance of pupils in kindergarten and night school classes In all other cases except for pupils
in high school departments no fees could be charged by the trustees
of any school district on account of the attendance of any children
whose parents or lawful guardians were ratepayers of the school
district [7]

In 1900 it was found that the majority of School Districts as at
first organized to meet existing requirements embraced the full twenty
five square miles of territory permitted by the School Ordinance, and
that owing to the limited amount of taxable land and the sparsity of
children of school age the boundaries of these districts were not contiguous As the country became more densely settled there came a
demand, particularly from the people living between established districts, for school accommodation in smaller areas

The increase in population through the influx of settlers, and the
rapid extension of railways in the province through the building of
many branch lines, with the railway townsite frequently located at
some distance from the centre of the district, occasioned no small
amount of difficulty in connection with the adjustment of the boundaries of school districts and the alteration of their limits This was
partly due to a demand for new schools more convenient to the new
centres of school population Then too, many ratepayers who owned
land adjacent to some rising hamlet found that the taxes in their districts were somewhat higher than in the purely rural districts adjoining, and frequently took steps to have their lands withdrawn from
the village district and included in the rural district This necessitated the alteration of many district boundaries

In Ontario and Manitoba the power to deal with this question
of alteration of boundaries of school districts is vested in the Municipal or County Councils and we believe rightly so, as they are more
thoroughly acquainted with local conditions and are thus able to
determine more justly what would be a fair apportionment of the
disputed territory

In the North West Territories it was necessary owing to the
absence of local municipal organizations or institutions, for the
Council of Public Instruction to deal with these matters directly
This necessitated considerable delay, owing frequently to the difficulty in securing accurate or satisfactory information by correspondence from the trustees or other ratepayers interested in the changes

---

6   *Ordinances of North-West Territories, 1896,* s 96
7   *Ibid, 1896,* s 106

involved Frequently it was necessary to delay action until an
inspector could be sent to investigate and make a report thereon

The number of school districts organized in the North West
Territories in the nine years from 1896 to 1904 inclusive was 40, 21, 22,
51, 49, 83, 119, 166 and 237 respectively [8] This is evidence not only of
the growth of settlement in the Territories but also of the interest
taken by the early settlers in educational matters In 1905 down to
August 31st, there were 231 formed After 1901 all new school districts
were established by the Commissioner of Education, who as head of
the new Department of Education, was one of the members of the
Executive Council

As early as 1883 the Lieutenant Governor had authority to dis-
organize any school district on any of the following facts being
established

 (a) failure to employ for at least three months in each year
a duly qualified teacher at a salary of not less than three hundred dollars per year,

 (b) failure to elect and keep in office a duly qualified Board
of Trustees,

 (c) failure to pay the debentures authorized for the building
of the school as agreed upon

In 1888 clause (a) was amended to read "Failure to open and
keep open the school for at least six months each year "

Upon the disorganization of a district the Chairman of the Council of Public Instruction or later the Commissioner of Education had
authority to appoint one or more persons as commissioners to settle
and dispose of the assets and property of such district and to make
the necessary financial adjustments

To prevent the education of the children being neglected in any
area of the province not exceeding five miles in length or breadth,
through the indifference of their parents, the Commissioner of Education had power to erect such area into a school district provided that
it contained

 (a) twenty children between the ages of five and sixteen
years inclusive,

 (b) ten persons actually residing therein who on the erection of the district would be liable to assessment,

 (c) six thousand acres of assessable land

Notice of the erection of any such district was required to be
published in the official gazette The Commissioner then appointed
some person to call a meeting of the resident ratepayers to elect
school trustees, such trustees to meet within ten days after their
election to organize a school board

If clauses (b) and (c) were fulfilled but there were not the number
of children required by clause (a) the Minister might order the area

----

8 *Annual Report, Department of Education, 1903*, p 12

to be erected into a school district if it were in the public interest
to do so

During the year 1906, the Department found it necessary to
appoint an official trustee to erect such school districts among the
Galician settlements, owing to the lack of acquaintance of these people
with the English language This policy which worked very satisfactorily was extended to other settlements with a foreign population
and is still in force The number of official trustees at the beginning
of the year 1925 was 40 and at the close of that year 52 For the
most part these are appointed in districts where it is not possible to
organize a board of trustees It is seldom necessary to replace a
board of trustees with an official trustee The young men and women
in the foreign settlements are now assuming the reins of office and as
they can speak English they usually perform their duties fairly efficiently

The early years of the Province gave ample evidence of an increased interest and healthy development in both elementary and
secondary education On September 1st, 1905, when the province
was established there were in existence 896 school districts [9] During
the years 1906, 1907 and 1908 there were organized 248,246, and 315
new districts respectively, an increase of nearly one hundred per cent
in three years [10]

These were busy times in the Department as the erection of so
many new districts necessitated, in many instances, the alteration and
adjustment of the boundaries of existing districts, as many of these
had been formed to secure the requisite number of children, and
without thought for the future development of the country This
necessarily occasioned a vast number of adjustments and alterations
in order that the boundaries of the new districts might be made to
conform with the boundaries of those previously erected During the
year 1907 there were some 72 alterations made by the Department in
the boundaries of existing districts As it was important that this
should be done in a manner to satisfy all parties concerned the
Government in 1906 appointed an inspector of school districts whose
special work was to visit the districts in question, to ascertain the
actual conditions, and to report thereon for the guidance of the Department

To provide for the education of the children in sparsely settled
areas of the province when there were more than five but fewer than
twelve children, a condition rendering it impossible to maintain the
average attendance required to earn the full grant, a district might be
organized for the purpose of conveying these children to the school
of an adjoining district [11] Or if an organized district had too few
pupils to warrant the operation of a school the attendance of the
children at an adjoining school might be arranged for, either by conveyance, in vans or by the parents, or by boarding them the cost
being paid by the district If the children were conveyed, the
Government paid one-third of the cost The board of any district

<hr>

9   *Report of Department of Education, 1904-1905,* p 27
10   *Ibid, 1908,* p 7
11   *Statutes of Sask, 1914*

had power to make due provision subject to the regulations of the Department as above stated for the proper conveyance of the school children resident within the district to and from school, and had power to provide for the cost of such conveyance in the same manner as was provided for the other expenditures of the district   This was a very wise and beneficial regulation in a new and sparsely settled province

Provision was also made in the session of the Legislature in 1912-1913 for the erection of "large" districts or for the consolidation of existing districts where deemed to be in the public interest, for the purpose of conveying children to a central school [12]   There are forty of these large districts, the largest of which comprises seventy-six and a half square miles and the smallest thirty-six and a half square miles.   In these districts conveyance of the children is compulsory and the Government through an amendment to the School Grants Act assists the extra cost of operation by the payment of a special grant of one-third of the actual cost of conveyance [13]

During the year 1919 there was organized within the Department of Education a School District Organization Branch with an Inspector in charge   This branch is held responsible for the administration of the school law as it applies to the erection of new school districts, alteration of boundaries of existing districts, the selection, approval and expropriation of school sites, the election of trustees, and other matters closely associated therewith

In 1921 the Minister of Education issued 534 orders providing for alterations in the boundaries of school districts   Many of these alterations were required because of the organization of new districts A large number were issued to provide new school districts centring on new villages, but the majority were approved by rural municipal councils to give better educational facilities to the particular children affected

There continues a steady demand for assistance in forming new districts in the newer areas of the province as well as in the older portions where it is often desirable that additional districts be formed by withdrawing lands from existing districts   School boundaries in the province are not considered fixed or permanent but may be altered at any time for good reason by transferring a parcel of land from one district to another   In 1927 the boundaries of 406 districts were altered in some degree for the greater convenience of the children affected [14]

---

12   *Report of Department of Education, 1913*, p 9
13   *School Grants Act, 1913*
14   *Report of Minister of Education, 1927*, p 13

VIII CONSOLIDATION OF SCHOOLS.

In the session of the legislature in 1912-1913 a radical amendment to the School Act made provision for the organization of large school districts, and for the consolidation of existing districts where it was deemed to be in the public interest Large districts of not less than thirty-six square miles nor more than fifty square miles might be formed, and in such cases the duty of providing for the expense of conveying to and from a central school once a day, each way, of the children of school age residing more than one and one-half miles distant, was laid upon the trustees [1] The School Grants Act was amended to provide for such schools a grant not exceeding one-third of the actual cost of conveyance Nine areas took advantage of these regulations and were organized as large districts during that year

During 1914 and 1915 little progress was made with consolidation, due partly to the sparseness of population and partly to the long distance children had to be conveyed which entailed an excessive expense The law at this time did not allow an area of more than fifty square miles to be consolidated, but owing to a growing demand for a larger area an amendment to the Act in 1917 gave the Minister of Education power under special circumstances to allow a larger area than fifty square miles to be included in a consolidated district. The clause was amended to read, "36 square miles or more" The chief objections raised to this were,

> (a) the difficulty of organizing van routes in sparsely settled districts and of securing van drivers,

> (b) the increased cost of operation, largely due to the cost of transportation of pupils

Owing to the different conditions existing in the various consolidated districts there is considerable variation in the rate of taxation required for the maintenance of these schools For example in 1919 in the rural areas of the districts the rate of taxation varies from $4\frac{1}{2}$ mills to 20 mills on the dollar and in the urban areas from 5 to 33 mills on the dollar The average cost of conveyance per pupil for a year varied from forty-four dollars to two hundred and eighteen dollars As high as nine dollars and fifty cents per day was paid for a van route During 1921 a number of the van drivers received better salaries than the teachers in the schools to which they conveyed the pupils

From the point of view of education no valid reason can be found against consolidation, but on the side of the cost of this plan of school administration there is evidently every reason to give it very careful consideration before taking final action culminating in the issuing of debentures secured by the taxes of the enlarged area for

---

1 *Statutes of Saskatchewan 1912-1913*, s 167, a

the resulting school accommodation required. As a matter of practical policy, its purely business features require careful consideration

During the year 1919 six consolidated districts were organized,
resulting in the disorganization of seven small districts In 1920 ten
new consolidated districts were organized, and three in 1921, making
a total of thirty-nine at the end of that year At the end of 1926
there were forty in existence so that there has been little progress
made in consolidation during the past three or four years This is
chiefly due to the fact that the consolidated districts have found the
cost of transportation a heavy burden These forty consolidated
schools had in operation one hundred and thirty departments with
4,598 pupils enrolled, of which number 2,332 were conveyed to school
at an annual cost of $71 25 per pupil [2]

The regularity of attendance in the consolidated schools is very
satisfactory. The lowest average attendance is 85 03 per cent of the
enrolment and the highest 95 67 per cent

The smallest area comprised in any of these consolidated districts is thirty-six and a half square miles and the greatest area is 76
square miles Sixteen of the school districts had an area greater than
50 square miles

In the urban area of any of these districts the lowest rate of
taxation was 9 5 mills and the highest 45 mills with an average rate
of 16 mills, while in the rural area the figures were 8 and 28 1 mills
respectively, with an average rate of 13 9 mills

The district having the largest enrolment of pupils, 311 in an
eight-room school has an area of fifty-four and one quarter square
miles and has been in existence since 1913 Its rate of taxation is 17
mills in both urban and rural areas 130 pupils were conveyed to
school at a total cost of $6,277 50 The total operating expenses of
the school were $26,142 48 and the Government grants to the district
were $6,012 16 The average attendance was 89 9 per cent of the
enrolment The smallest enrolment at school in any of these districts
was 36 pupils, in a rural area, all of whom were conveyed to school
from an area of 47 square miles at a total cost of $2,854 50, or an
average of $79 30 per pupil This is a one-room school and the
regularity of attendance was 88 62 per cent Another rural district
conveyed 30 pupils at a total cost of $4,043 75, or an average cost of
$134 79 per pupil This district was consolidated in 1917 and its
rates of taxation are 10 2 and 11 3 mills [3]

The total grants paid by the Government to the forty districts
for conveyance of pupils in 1927 were $52,979 79, which is approx-
imately one-third of the amount paid by these school districts for
conveying pupils during that year

There does not seem to be any tendency to increase the number
of consolidated school districts although those in existence are operating efficiently and to the general satisfaction of the ratepayers Financial considerations, including the high cost of conveying the pupils,

2 *Annual Report Department of Education, 1927*, Statistical Table, p 39
3 *Ibid ,, 1927*, p 39.

have apparently been the main factors in preventing further extension

Permissive legislation has been enacted which provides for the operation of what would be, in effect, (if not technically so) Municipal High Schools. A rural municipality may make a "maintenance grant" not exceeding in amount one thousand dollars per annum to a school or schools undertaking high school work. The recent regulations permit the council of any rural, village, or town municipality to pay to such a school the fees of all pupils attending from the municipality, or it may grant in lieu of fees a sum limited only by the discretion of the council.[4] Thus by co-operation between a municipal council and a school board the people of a municipality may decide for themselves just how far they will go in developing secondary education as a municipal undertaking. The initiative in promoting this type of co-operation will usually have to be taken by the school boards

Other permissive legislation enables two or more school districts to enter into contract with one another for the education of their students above Grade VII.[5] This applies to two or more rural districts or to rural districts adjoining a town or village district, to unite therewith to maintain a high school. This is a provision which has in it large possibilities for the development of secondary education in this province and already three such service centres have been established

One of the best examples of this co-operation is exemplified by the Town School District of Delisle which entered into an agreement for five years with seven adjoining rural districts, by which, on payment of certain amounts annually by the rural districts, the high school pupils of such rural districts have the right to attend the high school at Delisle to pursue the work required in Grades IX to XII inclusive. The amounts per pupil payable by the rural districts are based on the assessments in the district and vary from one hundred and fifty dollars to two hundred and thirty dollars annually. The extent of the co-operation under this clause is limited only by the mutual agreement of the boards and the approval of the Minister of Education. Thus very wide powers are given to school boards and municipal councils, i e , to the people in the local districts, to make adequate provision for municipal high schools, either by establishing continuation schools or high schools on a co-operative basis

Upon petition to the Minister of Education signed by the chairman and secretary of each district concerned, three or more adjacent rural school districts, the schools of which are closed from the twenty-second day of December to the fifteenth day of March, may be granted permission to co-operate to establish a community school.[6] A school board comprised of the chairman of each school district included is given authority and power to administer and maintain a community school in accordance with the regulations of the department

---

4 *Rural Municipalities Act*, s 173, s s 7, 8, 9.
5 *The School Act*, s 204, b
6 *Statutes of Saskatchewan, 1928*, c 48, s 14

The community school board is required to decide upon a rate of taxation sufficient for maintaining the community school, to be levied over the co-operating school districts, and to advise each municipal council concerned of such rate, and to make requisition for the amount of taxes required

In any school operating under the School Act the work of Grades IX and X was formerly required to be taught if demanded by any student of school age, unless the board had made provision for instruction of such student elsewhere, but this clause was repealed in the session of the Legislature of 1928 and it is now provided "that subject to the regulations of the department, the teaching of any grade above grade eight shall be optional with the board of trustees of the district [7]

<hr>

[7] *Statutes of Saskatchewan, 1928,* s 48, s 18 , *and*
School Act, s 202, s s 2

IX SECONDARY EDUCATION

As early as 1888 in order to meet a general demand from the larger centres of population in the Territories for more advanced education, provision was made for the establishment of classes in the elementary schools in which the higher branches of learning might be taught These were really continuation classes, but at that time were designated ' Union Schools " Before 1891 Union Schools had been organized in seven of the larger centres of population The principal of a Union School was required to be a graduate in Arts of some University in Her Majesty's Dominions, and to be capable of training teachers according to the most approved methods of teaching This type of organization possessed some features which made it very satisfactory in meeting the conditions and requirements of a new and sparsely settled country

After the formation of the new province and as the population increased there arose a growing demand for still better facilities for higher education This demand resulted in the passing of the "Secondary Education Act", which provided for the organization and maintenance of secondary educational institutions in the province It was assented to April 3, 1907 [1] By this Act any town or city municipality was given power to pass a by-law for the establishment of a high school within the municipality and for declaring such municipality to be a high school district where it could be shown to the satisfaction of the Department that such district could conform to the regulations respecting accommodation, attendance, library, equipment and apparatus The boundaries of high school districts were coterminous with those of the urban municipalities in which they were situated

All secondary educational institutions were placed under the control, management, and supervision of the Department of Education and made subject to such regulations of the Department as were approved by the Lieutenant Governor in Council, but no regulation could be adopted, amended, or repealed until it had been referred to the Educational Council for its discussion and report thereon

In compliance with the regulations, six High School districts were established in 1907, viz , Regina, Moosomin, Prince Albert, Moose Jaw, Weyburn, and Qu'Appelle This number had increased to 14 in 1911 with an enrolment of 1683 students, and to 24 in 1921 with an enrolment of 6903 pupils [2]

Each high school district elects its own board of trustees consisting of five members who hold office for two years or until their successors are elected [3] Every resident ratepayer of the district is qualified to serve as a member of the board

---

1 *Statutes of Saskatchewan, 1907*, c 25
2 *Report of Department of Education, 1921*, p 45
3. *Statutes of Saskatchewan, 1907*, c 25, s 10, 11

Every high school was required to admit any pupil whose parents or guardians were residents of the province and who had the necessary qualifications for admission as prescribed by the regulations of the Department without being required to pay tuition or other fees, except these resident in any town or village school district   These might be required to pay a fee not exceeding one dollar per month per family [4]

The revenue necessary for financing the secondary schools was secured partly from legislative grants paid largely out of the Supplementary Revenue Fund, and partly from the council of the municipality which provided its share of the money by the imposition of a high school tax rate levied on the same property throughout the district as the general taxes for municipal purposes were assessed [5]

The course of studies for high schools was fixed by regulations of the Department of Education and embraced instruction in English and rhetoric, commercial education, ancient, mediaeval and modern history, the natural sciences, mathematics and physics, the ancient and modern languages and such phases of university work as might be determined upon   To these subjects there have been added, instruction in agriculture, household science, manual, industrial and physical training, music, and art, with provision for such other subjects as may from time to time be determined upon.[6]

The payment of grants to High Schools was based partly upon the number of teachers employed, the number of teaching days the school was kept open, the character and extent of the equipment, apparatus, and library, the efficiency in respect to building, grounds, etc , and the report of the Inspector upon the efficiency of instruction   In accordance with the terms of The Secondary Education Act grants to High Schools and Collegiate Institutes were at first paid on the following bases

High Schools—

For each teacher employed, $1 25 per diem,
For equipment, apparatus and library $150 00 per annum until maximum equipment is provided, and thereafter $100 00 per annum,
On Inspector's report as to grading of school $200 00 per annum
For Commercial Course, $100 00 per annum,

Collegiate Institutes—

For each teacher employed, $1 50 per diem,
For equipment, apparatus and library $200 00 per annum until maximum equipment is provided and thereafter $150 00 per annum,
On Inspector's report as to grading of school, $300 00 per annum,
For Commercial Course, $100 00 per annum

---

4   *Statutes of Saskatchewan, 1907*, c 25, s 49-51
5   *Ibid , 1907*, c 25, s 37, 38
6   *Revised Statutes of Saskatchewan, 1920*, c 109, s 6

In addition, ten per cent of the money collected under The Supplementary Revenue Act, 1907, was divided among the several high schools and collegiate institutes

To be entitled to any grant provided by the Act every High School was required to have an average attendance of at least 25 pupils, and every Collegiate Institute of at least 50 pupils who had passed the Grade VIII examinations

The maximum number of days for which any per diem grant was paid, could not exceed 200 in any calendar year [7]

TABLE V   GRANTS PAID BY THE GOVERNMENT TO HIGH SCHOOLS AND COLLEGIATE INSTITUTES FOR THE YEAR 1908 [8]

	Under Secondary Education Act				Under Supplementary Revenue Act	Total
	1st term	2nd term	Equip'nt	Inspect'n		
Coll Institutes						
Regina	$ 915 00	$ 560 25	$ 200 00	$ 198 00	$2,458 75	$4,332 00
Moose Jaw	586 25	569 25	200 00	183 00	2,121 25	3,659 75
High Schools						
Moosomin	457 50	292 50		110 00	1,200 00	2,060 00
Pr Albert	455 00	197 50	125 00	92 00	1,044 00	1,913 50
Weyburn	297 60	197 50	100 00	126 00	316 00	1,037 10
Qu'Appelle	292 80	264 60	106 00	100 00		763 40
Saskatoon	302 50	281 25		106 00	934 00	1,623 75
Carlyle	Not open	196 00	40 00	37 60		273 60
	$3,306 65	$2,558 85	$ 771 00	$ 952 00	$8,074 00	$15,663 10

By the end of 1909 there were eight high schools districts established in the province and in two of these the schools were raised to the rank of Collegiate Institutes by order of the Lieutenant Governor in Council [9] In the Collegiate Institutes the following courses of study were given, viz., a General Culture course, a Teachers' Course, a Matriculation or University Course, a Commercial course, and a course in Agriculture

Schools doing the work of secondary education were known as Collegiate Institutes, High Schools and Continuation Schools The Continuation Schools were schools organized under the clauses of the School Act, while High Schools and Collegiate Institutes were organized under the Secondary Education Act, and were managed by a separate board of trustees designated the ''High School Board ''

7   *Statutes of Saskatchewan 1907*, c 25, s 61, 62
8   *Annual Report, Department of Education, 1908*, p 10
9   *Ibid , 1908*, p 10

There are thus three types or groups of schools which do high
school work, viz

Group A High Schools or Collegiate Institutes organized
under the Secondary Education Act In 1919 there were 24
high school districts but since 1921 five of these have been disorganized and are at present operating under the School Act and
are administered by the Public School Board of the district

Group B School districts organized under the School Act
and operating one or more rooms exclusively for pupils above
Grade VII If the room doing high school work contains also
the Grade VIII pupils it is known as a "Continuation School",
but if it is used exclusively for pupils beyond Grade VIII it is
called a "High School' This type of school has been gradually
increasing both in number and in enrolment of pupils

Group C Elementary school districts in each of which one
or more pupils are pursuing high school work chiefly that of
Grades IX and X These are mostly one-room rural schools and
receive the regular grant of $1 50 for every teaching day upon
which the school is legally open Continuation classes besides
receiving the grant of $1 50 per day are also granted an extra
three dollars per teaching day if there is an average attendance
of at least fifteen pupils, and no high school is in operation in
the district [10]

The increase in enrolment of pupils in secondary grades in the
different types of schools as indicated in "Table VI " denotes a rapid
growth in the number of pupils continuing their education beyond
Grade VIII The most pronounced increase being in the elementary
schools operating under the School Act The enrolment in the high
schools working under the Secondary Education Act reveals a decrease since 1921 when 6,903 pupils were enrolled in 24 high school
districts This indicates a very commendable desire on the part of the
people in the small towns and rural communities, to give their children a high school education without sending them far from home

TABLE VI   ENROLMENT OF PUPILS IN SECONDARY GRADES [11]

		No of Districts Operating 1927	Enrolment of Pupils			
			1908	1916	1924	1927
A	High Schools	19	734	3849	6726	6785
B	Continuation Classes	321	663	2593	6777	9210
C	Rural Elementary Schools	1556	180	663	2511	4123

10   *School Grants Act, 1920, s 3*
11   *Reports of Department of Education for years mentioned*

Up to 1907, the year in which the Secondary Education Act was passed, all secondary education was carried on in schools of types B and C

By reference to "Table VI" we see that in 1927 there were 13,333 high school pupils in schools organized under the School Act, and 6,785 in high schools organized under the Secondary Education Act

The Deputy Minister of Education in his report for 1927 makes the following statement in regard to these schools [12]

"Under The School Act, there were 435 rooms maintained for high school grades, 194 of these being classified as high school and 241 being rooms in which Grade VIII was also enrolled The latter are generally referred to as continuation rooms These continuation and high schools under The School Act, receive the same rate of grant as high schools under The Secondary Education Act They are to be found in practically every small town, village, and rural centre and are in effect rural high schools serving the rural communities They may be assisted financially by grants from the municipal councils, and adjoining school districts may likewise contribute annually toward their support In addition to the above, some 1556 schools mostly rural, gave some instruction in high school subjects"

As these schools are well distributed throughout the province, there is no well-settled district in which the children are far removed from a school offering the work of the secondary grades

By an amendment to the Secondary Education Act, which came into force on July 1st, 1926, fees may now be charged for high school education, but not exceeding twenty five dollars per annum in the case of the children of resident ratepayers of the district and of fifty dollars per pupil in the case of non-residents It is optional with any school district whether fees are charged or not in case of either resident or non-resident pupils, and in addition in the case of non-residents the fee may be paid by the school district or municipality where such pupils commonly reside [13]

The object of these amendments was to place all schools doing secondary education work on the same basis by making the fees exactly the same in all classes of schools, but always keeping in mind that the option remains with the municipality whether it will charge a fee or not It was also the desire of these amendments to further extend the facilities for secondary education to the country districts, to provide for the pupils in rural areas many of the educational advantages enjoyed by town and city students.

12   *Report of Department of Education, 1927*, p 13
13   *Secondary Education Act, Statutes of Saskatchewan, 1927*, c 34 s 49

X ADMINISTRATION OF SCHOOL GRANTS

The North West Territories Acts of 1875 and 1877 contained no clauses relating to schools or education

The first ordinance providing for the organization of schools in the Territories was passed in August 1884 but before being put into operation it was amended by the new ordinance of December 1885 By this ordinance specific grants to aid schools were adopted on the following bases

(1) on teachers' qualifications,

(a) $250 annually to each school employing a teacher with a third class or a provisional certificate,

(b) $300 annually to each school employing a teacher with a second class certificate,

(c) $350 annually to each school in which a teacher with a first class certificate was employed

Schools which were kept open for only one term were entitled to a proportionate share of these grants calcaulated according to the number of months during which the school was kept open,

(2) on attendance,

(a) $2 00 per child per annum to every school which had an average attendance of at least eight pupils, for every child who attended school 100 days, where school was kept open only for one term;

(b) $2 50 per child per annum to every school having an average attendance of at least eight pupils, for every child who attended 160 days where the school was kept open during winter and summer terms,

(3) on the Inspector's reports of the school, an annual grant of an amount not exceeding the total amount of the capitation grant for attendance, if the Inspector reported favorably on the work of the school

(4) for additional teachers,

(a) to every school district where the average daily attendance exceeded forty, a sum of $150 for an assistant teacher,

(b) to every school district where more than one assistant teacher was employed and where the average daily attendance was at least twenty pupils for each teacher, a grant of $100 for every assistant employed after the first

(5) for advanced classes,

To every district employing a teacher holding a first class certificate a grant was given to one group of pupils examined in the same

subjects, not being more than two subjects, at the rate of one dollar
per child, per subject

By the ordinance of 1888 a definite percentage of the teacher's
salary was assured to each school district, the grants being distributed on the following bases

(1)   to every school having a daily average attendance of not
      less than six pupils there was granted 75 per cent of the
      teacher's salary if the teacher held a first class certificate,
      70 per cent of salary of teacher holding a second class
      certificate and 65 per cent of salary for a teacher with a
      third class certificate,

(2)   grant for regularity of attendance

In school districts where the number of children of school age on
the register did not exceed twenty-five, a grant was paid which varied
from sixty dollars to thirty-five dollars according as the average daily
attendance varied from 75 per cent to 50 per cent of the number of
pupils on the roll

(3)   Grants for additional teachers, where the average daily
      attendance was at least twenty for each teacher employed,
      were distributed on the same basis as stated in section one

These regulations were repealed in 1892 and the following substituted

(1)   a grant of 70 per cent of the teacher's salary if this did
      not amount to more than $360 00 for a teacher with a third
      class or a provisional certificate   Amounts of $25 00 and
      $50 00 additional were allowed for teachers with second and
      first class certificates respectively,

(2)   there was also an additional grant of five dollars for each
      pupil in excess of ten pupils in daily average attendance,

(3)   where more than one teacher was employed each depart-
      ment with a daily average attendance of not less than
      twenty pupils ranked as a school   There was also a provi-
      sion to prevent the amount of the grant to any school
      exceeding the actual salary paid to the teacher

The method of apportioning grants to schools was changed in
1895 to encourage the keeping of schools open for a longer period
during the year   According to the new ordinance there was paid
from and out of moneys appropriated by the Legislative Assembly for
schools, in aid of schools organized and conducted according to the
provisions of the ordinance, an amount calculated as follows [1]

"(a) to each school having an average attendance of at least six
      pupils for the days during which it had been open in any
      term, a sum of one dollar and forty cents for each day the
      school was open, but not exceeding 210 days in any year,

---

1   *Report of the Council of Public Instruction, 1896*, Appendix A

(b) for every pupil in average daily attendance an additional amount of one dollar and fifty cents per school year of two hundred and ten days,

"(c) to each school where a teacher was employed, who held a first class professional certificate, the sum of twenty cents for each day in the year, such teacher was actually engaged in teaching, and to each school where a teacher holding a second class certificate was so employed the sum of ten cents for each day in the year such teacher was actually engaged in teaching,

"(d) to each school attaining a minimum grading upon the report of its inspection, as prescribed by the Council of Public Instruction, on its efficiency in respect to buildings, equipment, government, and progress, a sum not exceeding fifteen cents, nor less than five cents may be paid according to such grading for each day (not exceeding two hundred and ten) on which the school was kept open during the year,

"(e) to any high school complying with the provisions of the ordinance and the regulations of the Council a special grant of seventy-five dollars per term "

This is the first mention of grants to high schools

The sum of the grants to be paid in any term under clauses (a), (b) and (c) was not to exceed seventy per cent of the salary actually earned by the teacher during the term

In schools where more than one teacher was employed, each department ranked as a school under clauses (a) and (b) when the average attendance of the whole school equalled at least twenty pupils to each teacher employed No grant was paid to any school district until the bond required by the treasurer was received and registered by the Council of Public Instruction Grants might also be withheld from any school district where by reason of the neglect of the treasurer, teacher, or other official of the district, any returns as provided by the ordinance were delayed more than thirty days after the term or date otherwise specified for them to be forwarded to the Council, or it might be withheld if the officers of the district allowed their school to be conducted in violation of the provisions of the ordinance or of the regulations of the Council of Public Instruction, upon satisfactory evidence of such violation

Upon the recommendation of the chairman of the Council of Public Instruction, the Lieutenant Governor in Council might order the payment of a special grant to any school out of the general revenue funds of the Territories, whether the school was organized according to the law or not

The next important change in the system of distributing grants was occasioned by the passing of "The School Grants Ordinance" of 1901 By this ordinance the school districts were arranged into two classes, viz rural districts and village and town districts, and the grants payable to each class of school were computed on certain definite bases In rural districts they were based on [2]

- (*a*) the assessable acreage in the district A district of 6400 acres received a grant of one dollar and twenty cents per day for each day the school was kept open If the district contained more than the above fixed area, it received one cent less per day for each additional 160 acres or fractional part thereof The minimum grant under this clause was ninety cents per day If the district contained less than 6400 acres it received one cent more per day for each one hundred and sixty acres or fractional part thereof less than the fixed area,

- (*b*) the length of the school year A grant of forty cents a day was allowed for each additional day not exceeding fifty, the school was kept open in excess of 160 days during the year.

- (*c*) the certificate of the teacher A grant of ten cents per day was given to schools employing a teacher holding a first class certificate.

- (*d*) the percentage the average daily attendance bore to the enrolment The amount of this grant varied from five cents per day for a percentage of forty to fifty inclusive to twenty-five cents per day where the percentage exceeded eighty,

- (*e*) the grading of the schools as determined by the Inspector's report This was an annual grant of from five to fifteen cents per day based on a satisfactory report from the inspector of schools on the condition of the building, equipment, grounds, teaching and progress of the pupils At least one-half of this grant was required to be spent in purchasing books for a school library, or for equipment and apparatus

In town and village districts, the grants were distributed under somewhat similar provisions to those in rural areas

- (*a*) a grant of ninety cents per day for each day the school was kept open,

- (*b*) a grant of ten cents per day where a teacher holding a first class certificate was employed,

- (*c*) a third grant added five to twenty-five cents per day according to the percentage the average daily attendance bore to the enrolment,

- (*d*) a grant of from five to fifteen cents per day to each school receiving a minimum grading on its efficiency as based upon the Inspector's reports

An extra grant of seventy-five dollars per term was paid to each

----

2 *Report of Department of Education, 1902,* Appendix D and *School Grants Ordinance, 1901,* s 3

school maintaining one or more rooms exclusively for pupils above Grade VIII, provided the daily average attendance of pupils in such rooms was at least twenty during the term

In any district where more than one teacher was employed, each room ranked as a district or school for grant purposes, when the average attendance of the whole school was equal to at least twenty pupils to each teacher employed,

It was also provided

(a)   that grants should not be payable for more than 210 days in any calendar year,

(b)   that the total amount of the grants payable to any district should not exceed seventy per cent of the salary actually earned by the teacher

To every district providing the means of conveyance for children.from one district to a school in another district, the sum of sixty cents per diem was paid for each day upon which such conveyance was provided

This system of distributing grants seems to have worked most satisfactorily for it was continued in force after the organization of the North West Territories into provinces in 1905   Its most important advantages were

(a)   it encouraged the employment of teachers with the higher grade of certificate,

(b)   it tended to equalize taxation by the distribution of larger grants to the poorer or smaller school districts,

(c)   it encouraged regularity of attendance, as irregularity meant diminution of the amount of the grant earned,

(d)   it encouraged the trustees to keep the school open as long as possible during the year and to maintain the school building, grounds, and equipment in a fair state of efficiency,

(e)   it encouraged the establishment of a school library, which reacted to the benefit of the children

The very generous system of grants so encouraged the erection of new school districts that for several years there was a constantly increasing demand made on the treasury for their support   The number had increased from 896 in 1905, to 1,745 in 1909, and 2,898 in 1912

The school ordinances in force at the time of the organization of the province having proven satisfactory were continued without change, as the school system had been gradually developed not only to ensure the efficiency of the schools and the professional qualifications of the teachers but also to grant every possible assistance to school districts struggling with the difficulties incident to a new country

In 1907 owing to the increasing demand in many school districts for the teaching of the advanced work required for teachers' diplomas

and matriculation standing, the boards of trustees in these rapidly
growing centres were required to engage teachers holding high grades
of certificates and to provide increased equipment and apparatus to
secure proper instruction in the higher branches of study For this
extra expenditure in these graded schools for higher education, it was
felt that the grants being paid by the Department of Education were
entirely inadequate, so an Act called the "Secondary Education Act,"
was passed, which provided for the organization and maintenance of
secondary educational institutions in districts where it could be shown
to the satisfaction of the Department that such district could fulfil
the regulations respecting accommodation, attendance, equipment,
library, and apparatus The Department of Education maintained
the control, management and supervision of all secondary educational
institutions organized and maintained under and in accordance with
the provisions of this Act

The following grants were distributed to secondary schools [3]

(a) to every district maintaining a high school, one dollar and
twenty-five cents per diem for each teacher employed, not
exceeding two hundred days in one year;

(b) to every district maintaining a collegiate institute, one dollar and fifty cents per diem for each teacher employed,

(c) one hundred and fifty dollars per annum, to a high school
for equipment, apparatus, and library until the maximum
equipment prescribed had been provided, and thereafter
one hundred dollars per annum For collegiate institutes
the figures were two hundred dollars and one hundred and
fifty dollars respectively,

(d) an additional sum not exceeding two hundred dollars to
the high schools, and three hundred dollars to the collegiate institutes on the satisfactory grading of the school
as determined by the report of the school inspector,

(e) to every secondary school that made due provision for the
proper and regular instruction of pupils in the commercial
course prescribed by the high school course of study to
the satisfaction of the inspector, an additional grant not
exceeding one hundred dollars per annum was paid

For the purpose of supplementing the revenue of the Crown and
thereby providing increased grants for education "The Supplementary Revenue Act" was passed in 1907 by which there was levied in
each and every year, a rate of one cent per acre upon every owner
or occupant of land in the province (not comprised within the limits
of town and village school districts) for land owned or occupied by
him This rate was to be assessed and collected at the same time,
and in the same manner as the local improvement rates The net
amount of revenue produced under the Act was appropriated as
follows

(a) five per cent thereof for the establishment and maintenance of an agricultural college,

---

3 *The Secondary Education Act, 1907, and Report of Department of Education,
1908*, p 10

(b)   five per cent for the establishment and maintenance of the University of Saskatchewan.

(c)   ten per cent for the support of secondary educational institutions;

(d)   eighty per cent for the support of primary educational institutions

Out of the moneys set apart in support of secondary education, there was paid to every high school district in which a high school was maintained, the sum of two dollars per diem for each teacher employed, and to every high school district in which a collegiate institute was maintained, the sum of two dollars and fifty cents per diem for each teacher employed

Out of the moneys set apart each year in support of primary educational institutions, there was paid

(a)   five per centum thereof in support of rural school districts organized during the previous calendar year,

(b)   the sum of one hundred and twenty dollars to every rural district whose school was in operation at least sixty days during the previous calendar year,

(c)   to every school district maintaining an intermediate school as prescribed by the regulations of the department of education the sum of one dollar per diem for every teaching day such school was in operation during the previous calendar year

It was provided also that such grants should not be payable unless the trustees of the district admitted to the senior department of their school non-resident pupils, free of tuition and other fees

The data of Table VII shows the amount of the grants paid to schools for 1907, the first year in which the Supplementary Revenue Act was in force

TABLE VII.   GRANTS PAID TO ALL SCHOOLS FOR THE YEAR 1907

Class of School	No of Schools	No of Departments	Pupils Enrolled	Grants Paid Under the School Grants Ordinance		Supplementary Revenue Grant	Total Grants for 1907	Av Grant Per Pupil
				Ordinary Grants	Inspection Grants			
City	7	66	4,316	$15,024 93	$1,140 92		$16,165 85	$3 74
Town	43	134	6,679	28,758 20	1,823 20		30,581 40	4 58
Village	69	89	4,401	19,099 27	1,079 19		20,178 46	4 58
Rural	982	983	22,226	166,821 96	7,584 69	$142,480 66	316,887 31	14 25
	1101	1272	37,622	229,704 36	11,628 00	142,480 66	383,813 02	10 20
High Schools	4	11	246	1,066 25		1,760 00	2,826 25	11 49

NOTE —High Schools came into operation on September 1, 1907, under the Secondary Education Act

Foot Note—The total grants paid to schools in Saskatchewan in 1905 (the year in which the province was established) amounted to $157,468 45   This amount was distributed to 716 schools with 821 departments, an average per department of $191 80

The Legislature has made from year to year many changes in the different acts governing the administration of educational affairs in the province for the general purpose of facilitating the local authorities in establishing and maintaining their schools

During the first session of the Legislature of 1912-1913 an amendment to The School Act provided for the forming of large districts of not less than thirty-six square miles nor more than fifty square miles, and for the consolidation of existing districts where it was deemed to be in the public interest Provision was made for such schools to receive a grant not exceeding one-third of the actual cost of the conveyance of the pupils

The following year an amendment to the School Grants Act, made it possible for school districts having so few pupils of school age that it was impossible to maintain the average attendance requisite to earn the full grant, or to warrant the operation of the school, to convey the pupils to a neighboring school, under some local arrangement with the board of trustees of the neighboring district for teaching the pupils, and thereby obtain the grant for conveyance of the pupils as provided for consolidated schools. This made it possible for every child of school age in an organized district to be in regular attendance at some school In 1918 thirty-five school districts took advantage of this clause and conveyed their children to schools in neighboring districts

In 1914 the school fee of four cents per day per family paid by non-resident pupils to the board of trustees of the school attended, was increased to seven cents per day per family, or fourteen dollars and seventy cents for the full year of 210 teaching days This amount was not regarded as representing the average cost of education per family or even per pupil, but represented an average tax without constituting too great a financial burden upon the pioneer settler This tax was increased in 1919 to ten cents, and in 1921 to fifteen cents, which at present is the amount payable per day per family

In 1917 for the purpose of encouraging the teaching of secondary education in the small towns and villages, The School Grants Act was amended by adding to paragraph 2 of section 3 the following clause

"(a) an additional sum of $1 50 for every teaching day upon which there is maintained by the district during the year a school or room exclusively for pupils who have qualified for admission to high school in accordance with the regulations of the department, subject to the following conditions

(1) that the daily average attendance of pupils in such school or room is at least fifteen,

(II) that all such pupils are permitted to attend the school without payment of tuition or other fees,

(III) that the equipment provided and the instruction given is satisfactory to the department,

(IV) that the teacher in charge of such school or room holds at least a first class certificate "

This resulted in the establishment of a large number of well conducted continuation schools which have been a great assistance to the children in the rural sections of the province This clause of the Act was repealed in the session of 1918-1919 and the following substituted therefore

> "(d) An additional sum of $1 50 for every teaching day upon which there is maintained by the district during the year a school or room exclusively for the pupils above Grade VII, subject to the following conditions
>
>> " (1) that the daily average attendance of pupils in such school or room is at least fifteen,
>>
>> " (II) that the equipment provided, the classification of pupils and the instruction given are satisfactory to the department;
>>
>> "(III) that a high school or collegiate institute is not in operation within the district "

For the purpose of encouraging school districts to provide for the teaching of household economics a grant equal to fifty per cent of the initial cost of approved equipment but not exceeding twenty dollars (this was increased to thirty dollars in 1920) was authorised to be paid to a rural district where the board of trustees made provision for the noon lunch, or for giving instruction in household science

To each district establishing and maintaining a night school as per regulations of the School Act a grant of one dollar per evening session was authorised in 1918 for each teacher so employed In 1919, this grant was increased to two dollars per teacher for each evening session In 1921 this grant for night schools was withdrawn in districts having schools in operation under The Vocational Education Act [4]

The School Grants Act was amended in 1919 by adding a clause providing for a grant to rural districts for a teacher's residence, such grant not to exceed one-third of the cost thereof, and to be made by the Lieutenant Governor in Council after evidence had been furnished that such a residence was requisite for the proper operation of the school and also that without financial assistance from the province the district was unable to erect such residence In 1921 this clause was amended by fixing the sum of two hundred dollars payable to any rural district erecting an approved teacher's residence [5]

The year 1920 marks an important change in the distribution of grants to both elementary and secondary schools The Supplementary Revenue Act was repealed as it was felt that the amount of revenue available for grants from this source might steadily decrease

A new School Grants Act was adopted which made many variations and extensions to the provisions of the old Act on which it was

---

4   *Report Department of Education, 1921*, p 11
5   *School Grants Act, 1920*, s 3

based and substantially increased the grants formerly paid to both
elementary and secondary schools from all sources   The new bases
adopted by the new Act for the distribution of grants has remained
practically unchanged to the present time   In the new Act we no
longer find the following bases used in determining the amounts payable in grants to the school, viz

> (a) the grade of the teacher's certificate,
>
> (b) the amount of the teacher's salary,
>
> (c) the assessable acreage in the district,
>
> (d) the regularity of attendance,
>
> (e) the inspector's grading of the school (except in schools
> operating under the Secondary Education Act)

The Act provides for rural and village schools with not more than
five rooms in operation, the sum of one dollar and fifty cents per teaching day for each room, with additional sums of sixty cents and forty
cents per day for the first and second calendar years respectively that
the room is in operation [6]

In town districts the same grants were applicable, but as the
number of rooms increased the grants gradually decreased to ninety
cents per teaching day when more than twenty-five rooms were in
operation

In Continuation schools, that is, schools operating a room for
pupils above Grade VII, a special grant of three dollars per teaching
day was payable, provided that there was an average attendance of
fifteen pupils, thus making it possible for a continuation school to
earn a total grant of four dollars and fifty cents per teaching day for
the room in which high school work was carried on   This necessitated a very substantial increase in the amount of the grants distributed, particularly as the number of continuation schools had increased from twenty-one receiving grants in 1918 to the amount of
$6,551 63 to one hundred and ninety-seven in 1922, to which the sum
of $132,571 75 was paid in grants

The grants payable under the old Act, for the conveyance of
pupils to consolidated schools or to adjoining districts, for night
schools, for a teacher's residence, and for noon lunch equipment were
still continued in force

With the view of encouraging the installation of elementary
science equipment in schools where continuation classes were conducted, a grant was made to the district of fifty per cent of the initial
cost of such equipment but not in excess of twenty-five dollars
Town districts providing the minimum equipment for teaching science
in the first and second years, and physics and chemistry in the third
year of the high school course, were entitled to a grant of fifty per
cent of the initial cost of such equipment, such grant not to exceed
one hundred dollars

------

6 *School Grants Act, 1920*

TABLE VIII. COMPARATIVE STATEMENT OF GRANTS PAID TO PUBLIC
SCHOOLS FOR THE YEAR 1920 AND 1921.

	1920			1921	
	Regular Grants	Supp. Revenue Grant	Total	Regular Grant	Increase
Rural and Village School Districts open 210 days					
(a) 1st year in operation, 1 room.	$254.00	$103.14	$356.14	$441.00	$83.86
(b) 2nd year in operation, 1 room.	233.00	103.14	336.14	399.00	62.86
(c) Succeeding year	170.00	103.14	274.14	315.00	41.86
Town Districts open 210 days					
(a) 3 rooms in operation..	472.50		472.50	945.00	472.50
(b) 3 rooms in operation, one for work above Gr. VII .	787.50		787.50	1,575.00	787.50
(c) 7 rooms in operation, two for work above Gr. VII	1,732.50		1,732.50	3,171.00	1,438.50
(d) 11 rooms in operation, three for work above Gr. VII	2,677.50		2,677.50	4,431.00	1,753.50
(e) 21 rooms in operation in a high school area	3,307.50		3,307.50	4,851.00	1,543.50
(f) 100 rooms in operation in a high school district...	15,750.00		15,750.00	18,900.00	3,150.00

NOTE—(a) Possible additional grant per room in 1920 for first class teacher of
twenty-one dollars.

The Secondary Education Act, 1920, provided a grant of four
dollars per teaching day per teacher for high schools and collegiate
institutes. Previously they had received one dollar and fifty cents
per teaching day, supplemented by an amount varying from two dollars to two dollars and fifty cents per teaching day payable under the
Supplementary Revenue Act.

Every district whose high school received a satisfactory grading
by the inspector was paid a sum not exceeding two hundred dollars,
and if the school were a collegiate institute a grant not exceeding
three hundred dollars.

For each non-resident pupil in attendance in classes above Grade
VIII the sum of fifteen cents per diem was paid.

To every district whose high school was provided with the science
apparatus and library required by the regulations of the department
an additional grant of one hundred and fifty dollars per annum was
paid until the maximum equipment prescribed had been provided, and
thereafter while so maintained the sum of one hundred dollars per

annum   If the school ranked as a collegiate institute the grants were
two hundred dollars and one hundred and fifty dollars respectively

The very substantial grants distributed to school districts in
accordance with the provisions of the School Grants Act of 1920 in
support of both elementary and secondary education in the province
of Saskatchewan are not equalled by those of any other province in
Canada   This is very practical testimony of the importance which
the people of this province attached to education, and is indicative
not only of the rapid growth in the organization of school districts,
but also of the appreciation by the members of the legislature of the
necessity for liberal financial assistance to education under pioneer
conditions

The total amount distributed in grants to schools in 1915 was
$980,295 83, of which amount $790,968 56 was paid to rural schools,
and $189,327 27 to town, and city schools and to villages [7]   The 21
high schools received from Legislative grants during the same year
$70,348 64

In 1927, under the Schools Grants Act, the sum of $2,362,973 26
was paid in grants to schools organized under the School Act   To
high schools and collegiate institutes the sum of $147,871 28 was paid
under the Secondary Education Act and for vocational education
$37 892 52   Grants for teachers' residences amounted to $10,000 00

Out of the moneys appropriated by the Legislature for grants in
support of secondary schools at the present time, 1927, there is paid.[8]

    (a) to every district maintaining a high school or collegiate
institute $4 50 per diem for each teacher employed in teach-
ing Grades IX to XII inclusive   The maximum number of
days for which such grant shall be paid shall not exceed
200 in any calendar year,

    (b) to every district whose high school is provided with the
equipment, apparatus and library required by the regulations
of the department the additional sum of $150 00 per annum
until the maximum equipment prescribed has been provided,

    (c) to every district where a collegiate institute is provided
as in clause "b", the additional sum of $200 00 per annum

To be entitled to any of these grants every high school is required to have an average attendance for each school term of at
least 25 pupils, and every collegiate institute of at least 75 pupils who
have passed the Grade VIII examination or received standing equivalent thereto

---

7   *Report of Department of Education, 1915* p 23 24
8   *Ibid*, *1927*, p 14

TABLE IX   QUADRENNIAL STATEMENT OF GRANTS PAID IN SASKAT-
CHEWAN SCHOOLS 1886 TO 1926

Year	Schools in Operation	Pupils Enrolled	Teachers Employed	Total Grants Paid to Schools	Grant Per Pupil
1888	76	2,553	84	$ 8,908 72	$ 3 49
1890	195	5,389	224	85,002 45	15 77
1894	300	10,721	353	113,999 85	10 63
1898	426	16,754	483	133,642 79	7 98
1902	640	27,441	783	155 558 41	5 67
1906	873	31,275	1017	197,649 54	6 32
1910	1,912	63 964	2207	557,299 48	8 71
1914	3 055	111,059	3787	867 589 56	7 81
1918	3,941	147 232	4844	1,162,490 38	7 89
1922-23	4,322	187,968	5787	1,620,803 11	8 63
1926	4 506	205,962	6220	2,033,761 45	9 89

TABLE X   PER CAPITA EXPENDITURE AND RELATION OF GOVERNMENT
GRANTS TO TOTAL EXPENDITURE

Year	School Enrolment	Per Capita Expenditure	Total Expenditure	Government Grants	Percentage of Government Grants to Total Expenditure
1906	31,275	$54 36	$ 1,700,115 00	$ 174,218 00	10 24
1910	63,964	66 45	4,250,387 00	557,299 00	13 13
1914	111,059	85 65	9,512,249 00	867,590 00	10 85
1918	147,232	70 18	10,332,192 00	1,162,490 00	11 25
1922	178 314	79 70	14,211,999 00	1 779 228 00	12 52
1926	213 404	74 65	15,930,616 00	2 265 481 00	14 22

XI   DEBENTURE INDEBTEDNESS

Further evidence of provincial control of education is seen in the limitations placed by the Legislative Assembly on the power of school districts in borrowing money or contracting loans for the building and equipping of school buildings   By the School Ordinance of 1885, the school district became the unit of administration for school purposes with a large measure of local control, but boards of trustees were required to receive authority in writing from the Lieutenant Governor to contract a loan on the security of the school district if they had received the sanction of the ratepayers of the district by taking a vote thereon.   This money might be borrowed for the erection, purchase, or improvement of a school building, or for the the purchase or improvement of a school site, or for the purchase of suitable playgrounds for the children attending the school

All money was required to be borrowed by debenture, and the total face value of such debenture could not exceed one-tenth of the total assessed value of the real and personal property within the district, according to the last revised assessment roll of the district The debentures were not permitted to issue for a longer term than fifteen years if the school buildings were constructed of brick or stone, and for not longer than ten years if the buildings were of frame or log construction

The signing of these debentures by two trustees was sufficient to bind the school district and to create a charge or lien against all school property and rates in the school district for which such loan was made

By the school ordinance of 1896, the amount, which might be borrowed by debenture, was limited to one-tenth of the total assessed value of the real property within the district, and the debentures were not permitted to bear interest at a greater rate than eight per cent per annum, but they were allowed to run for twenty years if the school buildings were of brick, concrete, or stone, and for fifteen years if of frame or log construction

In 1901 educational affairs were placed under a department of the public service of the Territories called the Department of Education over which a member of the executive council appointed by the Lieutenant Governor in Council presided to discharge the functions of Commissioner of Education for the Territories   From this date until the Saskatchewan Act came into force in 1905, the authority for a school district to borrow money by debenture was authorised in writing by the Commissioner of Education and notice of such authorization was published in the official gazette

Certain changes were also made[1] which further restricted the amount of the debenture in rural districts so that the total face

---

1   *The School Ordinance 1901*, c 29, s 107-130

value henceforth could not be for a greater sum than twenty-five cents per acre for each acre assessed as shown by the last revised assessment roll of the district

The term of the debenture was changed for town districts so that the debenture thereof might now be drawn for a term not exceeding thirty years if the school buildings were of solid brick, stone or concrete and for fifteen years if of frame construction

The purposes for which money might be borrowed on debenture were extended to include the purchasing, adding to, or improving a site for a teacher's house, or for puchasing, repairing, erecting, furnishing, or adding to a teacher's house Thus the proceeds of the loans were laid out mainly on the construction and equipment of school buildings, the greater proportion of which were erected in rural areas at an average cost of about twelve hundred dollars during the earlier years of the history of the province Public opinion was so strongly in favor of well-equipped buildings of a permanent type that it became a necessary function of the department to restrain boards of trustees from incurring expenditure not justified by reasonable prospective needs of the school district It was thus able to exercise its right of control in the best interests of the district and to give assurance that the money borrowed by debenture was not used for the current expenses of the district contrary to the provisions of the school ordinance, but was actually expended for legitimate debenture purposes

As an index of the development of the province, as well as an evidence of the interest taken in education, the following statement of debentures authorised during the years immediately preceding and subsequent to the organization of the province is enlightening

TABLE XI   SCHOOL DISTRICT DEBENTURES

Year	No of School Districts	Amount Authorized
1898	39	$ 23,985 00
1900	61	94,500 00
1902	137	141,175 00
1904	291	493,365 70
1906	312	410,610 00
1908	354	620,740 00
1910		552,360 00
1912	457	2,435,120 00

In 1904 the amount of debentures authorized in the area included in the present province of Saskatchewan was $209,675 00

Debenture loans registered in 1908 amounted to $856,540 00, of which amount $160,000 was contracted by high school boards under the provisions of the Secondary Education Act [2] These being municipal loans they were authorized after the ordinary municipal procedure by the Council of the city or town municipality

2   *Annual Report Department of Education, 1908*, p 11, 22

The total debenture indebtedness of the province in 1908 was
$1,965,720 45, while the estimated value of all the school sites and
buildings with equipment was $3,017,631 64, and the excess of all
assets over liabilities of the school districts wsa $1,597,456 59 [3]

In 1913 Boards of Trustees of school districts, which comprised
within their limits a city municipality were empowered when borrowing money for the erection of a school building and the acquiring
of a site to issue a straight term debenture with provisions for a
sinking fund for retiring the same   The amount of the debentures
registered in 1913 was $2,979,400   As part of this sum forty-eight school
districts borrowed amounts of five thousand dollars or upwards [4]

An Act providing for the creation of a Local Government Board
was assented to at the meeting of the Legislature in 1913   This
board is composed of three members appointed by the Lieutenant
Governor in Council, one of whom is appointed as chairman, a position which he is entitled to hold as long as he continues a member
of the board   Each commissioner is entitled to hold office during
good behaviour for a period of ten years, and is eligible for reap-
pointment if not disqualified by age—seventy years

The board when first constituted was given the following powers [5]

(a) to inquire into the merits of any application of a local authority for permission to raise money by way of debenture, or
upon the security of stock, and to grant or refuse such permission,

(b) to manage notwithstanding anything in ' The City Act" or
the "Town Act" the sinking fund of any local authority
which desires to intrust the same to the board for
management,

(c) to supervise the expenditure of moneys borrowed by a local
authority under this Act,

(d) to obtain from any local authority at any time, a statement
in detail of its assets and liabilities and of its revenues and
expenditures for any definite period   When a local authority desires to provide for raising of a loan by way of
debenture or upon the security of stock for the purpose of
any work or undertaking, the acquisition of property or any
other object within its jurisdiction, it is required to make
application to the board for permission to do so

School Boards contemplating the erection of a new school are
required to submit the site under consideration to the Local Government Board for its approval, and where the amount of money to be
borrowed in town districts exceeds five thousand dollars, the board is

3   *Report of Department of Education 1908*   p 21
4   *Ibid , 1913,* p 14 15
5   *Revised Statutes of Saskatchewan, 1920,* c 23

also required to receive the consent of the Local Government Board
to the loan before submitting the same to the vote of the burgesses [6]
Any moneys received by a School Board for the purposes of a sinking
fund can not be devoted to paying any portion of the current or
other expenditures of the district The members of a school board,
who vote for the diversion of debenture moneys are personally liable
for the amount so diverted, which amount may be recovered by the
district by action against these trustees in the Court of King's
Bench, and the members who voted for the same are disqualified
from being elected members of a board of school trustees or from
holding any municipal office for a period of two years The School
Boards of rural districts situated in rural municipalities are empowered
to borrow on promissory notes such moneys as are required for the
payment of a debenture coupon

At present, 1927, the total value of all outstanding debentures
shall not at any time be for a greater sum than one-tenth of the
total assessed value of the assessable property of the district

Districts are also required to issue debentures in one of the following forms unless the approval of the Local Government Board
has been obtained to a different form

    (a) the principal to be repayable in equal annual instalments
       with interest annually or semi-annually upon the balances
       from time to time remaining unpaid,

    (b) the principal and interest be combined and be made repay-
       able in equal annual instalments,

    (c) in the case of a district comprising within its limits a city
       municipality, the principal be repayable at the end of a
       period of years with interest payable annually or semi-
       annually

In case debentures are issued in the form described in clause (c)
the district is required to raise annually by way of sinking fund a
sum sufficient with interest compounded half-yearly at four per cent
per annum to retire the debenture at maturity, and such sum must
be added each year to the amount of the other school rates and
taxes and collected therewith

Every debenture before being issued must be sent to the Minister for registration and proper record of the same When registered
and countersigned by the Minister or Deputy Minister, the legality
of the issue of the debenture is thereby conclusively established and
its validity is not questionable by any court in Saskatchewan, but it
is to the extent of the revenues of the district issuing it a good and
indefeasible security in the hands of any bona fide holder thereof [7]

---

6   *The School Act, 1928,* s 160-171
7   *Ibid , 1928,* s 172, 173

Year	Debentures Authorized		Debentures Registered	
	No of School Districts	Amount	No of School Districts	Amount
1898	39	$ 23,985 00	30	$ 20,433 00
1900	61	94,500 00	52	77,800 00
1902	137	141,175 00	123	114,900 00
1904	291	493,365 70	292	366,615 70
1906	312	410,610 00	312	399,930 00
1908	356	620,740 00	385	856,540 00
1910		552,360 00		628,129 80
1912	457	2,435,120 00	422	2,295 760 00
1914	314	1,360,125 00	324	1,178,300 00
1916	291	559,260 C0	327	649,300 00
1918	212	512,770 00	197	609,150 00
1920	381	2,460,508 00	241	1,594 985 00
1922			181	611,713 68
1924			141	530,321 63
1926			209	881,510 50

XII NORMAL SCHOOL TRAINING

The history of the Normal School in Saskatchewan is the history
of the origin and growth of a school system under pioneer conditions
in the North West Territories, and its subsequent development in the
two great provinces created within the same territory in 1905

On July 28th, 1886, the Board of Education of the Territories,
met with the honourable Thomas White, then Minister of the Inter
ior, in connection with a proposition that a High School, with a
Training School for teachers attached, should be erected at Regina
The Minister promised to give attention to the matter on his return
to Ottawa [1]

Inspector Thomas Groves, in his report[2] in 1886 on the Western
Assiniboia Protestant Schools, advises the Board of Education, that,

> "There are many teachers now holding Provisional Certifi-
> cates, who intend to follow the profession of teaching, and who
> would like to attend a Training and High School to fit them-
> selves for their profession, provided they could do so without
> incurring the additional expense of leaving the Territories "

In 1886 there were in the Territories, 65 Protestant schools
employing 67 teachers and having an enrolment of 2,041 pupils,
and 12 Roman Catholic schools employing 17 teachers with 512
pupils enrolled [3]

The Secretary of the Board of Education in his report of 1886-
1887 to the Lieutenant Governor, makes clear the attitude of the
Board with respect to teacher-training in the following statement [4]

> "The desirability of establishing some system of High
> Schools in the Territories, has frequently been under the con-
> sideration of the Board, and specially with a view to obtain in
> connection therewith an institute wherein our teachers could be
> trained in the science and art of teaching As directed a copy
> of the following resolution of the Board was forwarded to the
> Minister of the Interior on this subject, viz 'That this Board
> desires to urge upon the Federal Government the desirability
> of a grant of $30,000 00 being made to the North West Terri-
> tories for the purpose of establishing one or more High Schools
> and a Central Training School That the grant in aid of schools
> at present given is required for the common schools, and in con-
> sequence no provision can be made to encourage or establish
> High Schools "

---

1   *Report of Board of Education, 1886,* p 18
2   *Ibid , 1886,* p 27
3   *Report of Board of Education, 1886.* p 15
4   *Ibid , 1886-1887,* p 11

The Deputy Minister in acknowledging receipt of the letter transmitting a copy of the said resolution, stated that the subject would be dealt with in an official communication to the North West Council

In June 1887 the regulations with reference to the granting of certificates to candidates, who had had no Normal or Model School Training, were fixed by the Protestant Section of the Board as follows [5]

"Third Class Certificates

A candidates on passing the required examination for a 3rd Class Certificate will be granted a 3rd Class Non-professional certificate, valid for one year

On production of such certificate at the expiration of that time, endorsed by the School Inspector, the candidate will, subject to the approval of this Section of the Board, receive a 3rd Class Professional Certificate, under which he must teach for at least two years

"Second Class Certificate

On production of a 3rd Class Professional Certificate with two endorsements by the Inspector of Schools, and passing the required examination for a 2nd Class Certificate, a candidate will, subject to the approval of this Section of the Board, be granted a 2nd Class non-Professional Certificate, valid for *one* year.

On production of such certificate, at the expiration of that time, endorsed by the School Inspector, the candidate will, subject to the approval of this Section of the Board, receive a 2nd Class Professional Certificate, under which he must teach for at least one year

"First Class Certificate

On production of a 2nd Class Professional Certificate, endorsed by the School Inspector and passing the required examination for a 1st Class Certificate, a candidate will, subject to the approval of this Section of the Board, receive a 1st Class Professional Certificate, valid during good behavor

"Provisional Certificates

Provisional Certificates will be granted to teachers, not holding Normal School or any class of certificates, on their sending the following information to the Inspector of Schools for the District in which they desire to teach, viz

1 A recommendation from the Board of Trustees of the School District

2 Evidence of good moral character

3 Satisfactory evidence as to competency

5 *Report of Board of Education, 1886-1887*, Appendix E, p 51

4   An application for the certificate in the applicant's own
handwriting

Provisional Certificates shall only remain in force for one
year from the date of issue, but shall lapse sooner if the holder
shall fail to pass the examination for a 3rd Class Certificate
held during the year "

The first Teachers' Examinations for 2nd and 3rd Class Certificates in the Territories were held on the 11th, 12th and 13th days
of January, 1887

In 1888 the Board gave its approval to the establishment of
Schools for Higher Education [6]   This permitted the establishment of
departments for the teaching of High School subjects in those schools
where such a course was warranted by the number and the state of
advancement of the pupils   Schools organized to do this advanced
work were designated "Union Schools", and in March of 1889 the
Board adopted tentative and provisional regulations governing the
Entrance Examinations, and the Course of Study to be used in such
schools

The Head Teacher of every High School branch of a Union
School was required to be a graduate of some University in Her
Majesty's Dominions, or have attainments which, in the opinion of
the Board of Education, were equivalent thereto, and who was able
to satisfy the Board as to his knowledge and ability to conduct such
a school and to train teachers according to the most approved
methods of teaching

It was compulsory for every Union School to have a Normal
School Department,[7] which should hold one session each year, if
required to do so by the Board of Education   Every such session of
the Normal School opened on the first Monday in November and
closed on the last Friday of the following March   The course of
instruction during such sessions included the following subjects
The History, Science, and Art of Education, Methodology, School
Organization and Management, School Hygiene, School Law, Drill
and Calisthenics, Practical Teaching and as much as time permitted
of the work prescribed in the highest Standard for Protestant Schools,
or in the Superior Course for Roman Catholic schools   In 1890 it
became obligatory for the student to attend such classes as the
Inspector in his judgment deemed necessary

During 1889 Union Schools were organized at Calgary and Regina   In 1890 four more were established at Moose Jaw, Moosomin,
Lacombe and Prince Albert

The only existing official record of Normal training having been
given was that of the work done by Mr A H Smith, B A, principal
of the Moosomin Union School, who in addition to his other work,
lectured on the science and art of teaching to a number of students,
who had obtained second and third class non-professional certificates
This voluntary course ended April 8, 1890 [8]

6   *Report of Board of Education 1887-1888*, p 10
7   *Ibid, 1888-1889*, p 8
8   *Report of the Council of Public Instruction, 1896*, p 16

When organizing these Union Schools the Board of Education
gave expression to the feeling that in this experimental stage of Normal Training, that it had to rely very greatly upon the judgment
and good sense of Inspectors and Principals to make such arrangements as would result in the carrying on of a complex system with
the utmost advantage to all the pupils concerned, but evidently the
teachers in some of these Union Schools had been devoting too much
of the school time to the teaching of the professional subjects for we
find that in 1890 the Board passed the following resolution relating
thereto [9]

> "Resolved   That, whereas complaints have been made, that
> too much time is being devoted in Union Schools to the training
> of teachers, the Secretary be directed to issue a circular letter to
> the principals of the various Union Schools pointing out that the
> primary object of the High School Department is to afford
> instruction in the higher branches of education, and that the
> training of teachers is not part of the work of any Union School,
> until a Normal Department is authorized "

At the same time the Board by resolution established Normal
Departments at the Regina and Moosomin Union Schools to be conducted in each case by the Inspector of Schools for the District, i e ,
one school in West Assiniboia and one in East Assiniboia

The Board also promised to endeavor to organize Normal
Departments in other Inspectoral Districts whenever there were ten
holders of non-professional certificates who desired to receive Normal
training in any Union School

In 1891 the Board of Education made it compulsory for all persons who held non-professional certificates and who desired to teach
in the Inspectoral Districts of Eastern and Western Assiniboia to
receive adequate Normal training at either Moosomin or Regina
While the Board desired to extend similar advantages to the other
inspectorates under its jurisdiction, it could not do so as the schools
in these inspectorates were so few and so widely scattered

To meet the difficulty the Board submitted to the Lieutenant
Governor a proposition[10] made by it to the Authorities at Ottawa
in January 1888, in the following terms, viz

> "That in the opinion of the Board it is necessary to make
> provision for the instruction and training of teachers for our
> public schools in the Science and Art of teaching

> "That the Board feels that the appointment of a Normal
> School Principal, whose duty it would be to hold Normal Ses-
> sions in different parts of the country, would have the best
> possible results in increasing the efficiency of teachers and in
> stimulating education "

---

9   *Report of Board of Education, 1889-1890*, p 7
10   *Ibid , 1890-1891*, p 21

Therefore Resolved

"That His Honour the Lieutenant Governor be requested to urge upon the Dominion Government the advisability of granting the sum of five thousand dollars for the next financial year for Normal School purposes"

In the event of this suggestion receiving approval, the Board planned to secure the services of a competent Normal School Instructor and to make such provision for the holding of Normal Sessions at such places in the Territories as might from time to time appear to require them

In 1890 two Normal School sessions were conducted at Moosomin by Inspector Hewgill   The first ending April 8th, in which one 2nd Class and six 3rd Class candidates were trained, and the other ending December 23rd, in which six 3rd Class candidates received their training   In Regina no candidates presented themselves that year

There were no sessions in 1891, but in the early part of 1892 and 1893 sessions were conducted at Regina and Moosomin by Inspectors Rothwell and Hewgill respectively

The School Ordinances were amended and consolidated in 1892 and a Council of Public Instruction constituted, with power to establish Normal Schools   On April 1, 1892 Mr D J Goggin, M A , was appointed Director of Normal Schools, and in August of the same year the Council declared

"A non-professional certificate shall not be valid as a license to teach"[11]

This declaration made professional training compulsory on all candidates for a teacher's certificate

In 1893 the first regular Normal School was established at Regina with a special instructor in charge   Sessions for First and Second Class candidates were conducted annually therein beginning September 1 and ending December 22nd   Sessions for Third Class candidates beginning January 2 and ending March 15 in each year, were conducted at convenient local centres by the Inspectors under the supervision of the Director of Normal Schools, who delivered a course of lectures at each centre   This Normal School at Regina served the whole of the North West Territories until the creation of the Province in 1905

In 1893 there were in attendance at the Normal classes in Regina 18 First and 35 Second Class students, while in the first session of 1905, the last year of the Normal School as a Territorial Institution 20 First and 95 Second Class candidates were in training[12] In 1904 and 1905 owing to the growing demand for trained teachers, two sessions were held—January to April and August to December Subsequent to 1895 Third Class teachers received their training at Regina and Edmonton, while previous to that date they were trained at Moosomin, Calgary and Regina   In 1906 Alberta established her

11   *Report of the Council of Public Instruction, 1896* , p 17
12   *See Table XIII*, p 163

own Normal School at Calgary and the original in Regina became a Provincial Institution serving the needs of Saskatchewan until 1912, when a second Povincial School was opened at Saskatoon

Owing to the prevailing great demand for teachers occasioned by the rapid establishment of new school districts within the Province two Normal School sessions continued to be held each year at Regina

TABLE XIII   NORMAL TRAINING IN THE NORTH WEST TERRITORIES [13]

Sessions at Regina for training of 1st and 2nd Class Teachers			Sessions at Regina and other points For Training 3rd Class Teachers	
Number of Students Attending and Class of Certificate			Number of Students Attending	
Year	1st	2nd	Total	3rd Class	Totals
1893	18	35	53	9	62
1894	5	22	27	37	64
1895	9	13	22	18	40
1906	7	16	23	15	38
1897	12	37	49	38	87
1898	23	36	59	35	94
1899	18	58	76	25	101
1900	18	67	85	10	95
1901	25	73	98	18	116
1902	20	72	92	19	111
1903	27	93	120	3	123
1904	45	140	185	3	188
1905	20	95	115	12	127
	247	757	1004	242	1246

Trained at Normal Sessions held previous to 1893   55

Total -   - 1301

Students who had had no professional experience were admitted to these sessions, but in 1907 a new regulation was approved by the Department of Education whereby all persons, whatever their academic standing, were required to attend a Third Class session of the Normal School and to have at leeast one year's experience in teaching before being granted permission to attend the Provincial Normal School for training for a First or Second Class certificate

In the same year the age limit for admission to the Normal School was raised for male teachers to eighteen years and for female teachers to seventeen years

A reading course was also organized and all teachers holding Interim First or Second Class certificates were required to complete at least one year of the reading course before being granted permanent certificates   By this means it was hoped to stimulate the teachers to continue a systematic course of professional reading,

---

13   *Report of the Department of Education, 1904-1905*, p 32-35

which would result beneficially to the members of the teaching profession

The increasing demand for trained teachers made it necessary to provide more adequate accommodation for Normal School purposes so that in 1912 a contract was let for the erection of a Normal School building in Regina at a cost of approximately $200,000 00, situated on grounds of about ten acres in area very conveniently located within the City Though the structure was not fully completed, the winter session of 1914 opened on January 5th in this new Normal School Building with an attendance of 165 students [14]

For the Autumn session of 1912 a second Normal School was opened at Saskatoon Its sessions were held in different buildings throughout the City,[15] until January 1922, when a modern and thoroughly equipped building on a commanding site was opened as a teacher-training institution, in which ample provision was made for training in household economics, manual training, elementary science, nature study, agriculture and art, while spacious class rooms and auditorium accommodation provided for a rapidly growing student body

The number of students from the Secondary and Continuation Schools of the Province who have in recent years passed the necessary examinations qualifying them for admission to the Normal School has been so great that it became necessary to establish a third Normal School at Moose Jaw in September 1927 A new building more modern and adequate than that at Saskatoon is in course of construction and will be ready for occupancy by the Normal students at the Autumn session of 1929

To increase the supply of trained teachers and to lessen thereby the demand for provisional certificates, of which as many as 1346 had been issued in one year—1912, Third Class sessions of the Normal School were held at different centres in the Province, as well as the First and Second Class sessions which were held at Regina and Saskatoon in both the spring and autumn of each year

-----

NORMAL CLASSES FOR SPECIAL STUDENTS

For several years prior to 1914 there had been in operation in the old Legislative Buildings in Regina, a Training School for foreign students preparing for teaching in foreign-speaking communities The segregation of these students had not been found to be in the best interests of the students or of the phase of education concerned, consequently a change in the system was introduced in 1914 by which they were attached to the Provincial Normal School, Regina, and placed under the training of two experienced inspectors of schools Instead of being housed in one building they were permitted to choose their own boarding houses from lists approved by the Principal of the Normal School

-----

14   *Report of Department of Education, 1914*, p 33
15   *Ibid, 1919*, p 98

In this year some fifty one students were in attendance, of whom ·
thirty-eight were Ruthenians, three Austrians, three Russians, four
Germans, one Pole, one Icelander and one Canadian They received
a five months course of training in general methods and were given a
good foundation for teaching the various academic subjects of the
school course They also had the advantage of the excellent library
and reading room, and gymnasium of the Normal School, as well as,
the privilege of attending the lectures by the different members of the
Staff of the school They also had a joint literary society with the
Third Class students which promoted intercourse and exercised a
beneficial Canadianizing influence

Some of these students had not secured Grade VIII standing,
consequently a large proportion of the time was devoted to the
teaching of the academic subjects As students they made very satisfactory progress considering their previous attainments and the difficulties of language, etc , which some of them had to overcome The
majority of these students were engaged as teachers in foreign-speaking districts On the whole as teachers they did earnest, conscien-
tious work Their pupils made very fair progress in learning English,
and the discipline of their schools was invariably reported as excellent

In the fall session of 1919 the Normal School course for teachers
with First and Second Class academic standing was extended to 33
weeks This proved advantageous in permitting a better review of
the academic work viewed from the standpoint of methodology, in
giving more time for training in certain special subjects, such as,
music, manual training and art, and in giving more time for practice
teaching [16] In order that the practice teaching might be effectively
supervised several inspectors of schools were called in to each Normal
School from their inspectoral duties to act as critic teachers and to
help with the training of the students Their wide practical experience of rural classroom conditions rendered them very helpful critics
of the young inexperienced teacher They were also of valuable
assistance in helping to unify the practical and the theoretical phases
of the professional training The efficiency of the inspection of the
schools in their different inspectorates must naturally have suffered
from these extended periods of absence So that this practice has now
been superseded by a co-operative arrangement between the Department and the School Boards of the three cities interested, whereby
the regular teachers in charge of the classrooms visited by the students
act as critic teachers under the supervision of the Normal School
masters

The Department of Education in co-operation with the University of Saskatchewan has conducted Summer Courses at the University for several years in a number of subjects including professional training in Primary Methods and in Education The object
of these courses is to provide an opportunity for teachers to improve
their professional standing The training in Primary Methods enables the teacher to do her work more efficiently and to secure a
more desirable position Under the regulations governing the courses

----

16 *Report of Department of Education, 1919*, p. 94

in Education. teachers holding Second Class certificates and who
have First Class academic standing may qualify for an Interim First
Class certificate by attending the course in Education at the summer
school [17] The number of teachers who have taken these courses
during the years 1922 to 1927 inclusive is as follows

Course	1922	1923	1924	1925	1926	1927	Total
Primary Methods	21	31	42	75	61	93	323
Education	38	55	32	57	57	79	318

In September 1926 the Department of Education was unable
for the first time in the history of the Province, to accommodate
at the two Normal Schools all the students who sought admission
The immediate difficulty was overcome by opening six local training
centres for those students who wished to take the Third Class course
In the following January when the Department was compelled for
lack of accommodation to refuse admission to many students who
wished to complete their training for Second Class certificates it was
decided to abolish the Third Class sessions of the Normal School,
to extend the term of training from thirty-three to thirty-eight
weeks, and to raise the age of admission of all students to eighteen
years   No Third Class certificates will be issued henceforth by the
Department, and the practice of granting standing to Third Class
teachers from outside the province was discontinued [18] Arrangements however were made to allow those teachers who had taken the
Third Class Normal Course and who had First or Second Class
academic standing to complete their professional training for these
higher certificates by attending short courses of training at the
Normal Schools in the Spring and Fall of each year until June 1930

In regard to the present supply and training of teachers, the
Registrar of the Department of Education in the report of 1927
makes the following statement [19]

"In September 1927, the Department was unable to accommodate at the Normal Schools at Regina and Saskatoon all
the students who applied for admission   Steps had already been
taken by the Government to build a new Normal School in the
City of Moose Jaw   In the meantime, through the courtesy of
the Moose Jaw High School Board, arrangements were made to
open a Second Class session of the Normal School in the annex
to the Ross Collegiate Institute, and late in September this
class opened with 300 students in attendance

"Fewer teachers are now coming to the province from other
provinces and the teaching positions are being filled more and
more by graduates of our own Normal Schools   According to
the records of the Department, out of 1970 new licenses to teach

---

17   *Report of Department of Education, 1919,* p 58 and *Ibid, 1927,* p 88
18   *Ibid, 1926,* p 13 and 67
19   *Ibid, 1927,* p 86

issued by the Department in 1927, only 201 were granted to
teachers from outside the province Each year for the past four
years over 3000 students in our schools have qualified for admission to the Normal School by passing either the Grade Eleven
or the Grade Twelve examination

"This condition of affairs has enabled the Department to
raise the standard of the requirements for admission to the
Normal School and to abolish the Third Class Normal School
Sessions "

The training received in the Normal Schools has exacted a continuing beneficent influence on the life and development, and
the growth and prosperity of Western Canada Looking back over
the past thirty years it may well be said that no institution has
better filled its appointed place in the community than has the
Normal School

Table XIV showing the number of teachers who have been
trained in the Normal Schools of Saskatchewan from 1906 to 1926
inclusive indicates that since 1921 the percentage of teachers who
have received their academic standing in the Province is becoming
increasingly a higher percentage of the total teaching body, so that
Saskatchewan can now depend upon her own educational institutions
to supply the demand for new teachers

TABLE XIV   NORMAL SCHOOL STUDENTS—1906-1926 INCLUSIVE

WHERE ACADEMIC STANDING WAS OBTAINED [18]

	Sask	Man	Ont	Que	N S	N B	P E I	Alta	B C	Nlfd	Great Britain	U S A	Other c'n'r's	Total
First Class														
1906-1911	42	10	39	0	6	0	3				1			101
1912-1916	314	54	106	8	21	3	3	2	1		29	8		549
1917-1921	335	46	49	2	13	1	3	3	2		6	3	3	466
1922-1926	977	85	63	3	22	9	1	5	3		10	5	3	1186—2302
Second Class														
1906 1911	254	55	270	7	19	5	7				7			624
1912-1916	451	151	142	12	28	14	7	1		1	65	16	1	889
1917-1921	1061	219	110	7	55	10	20	19	1	1	41	50	1	1595
1922 1926	1926	291	66	16	29	12	43	20	4		91	55	2	2555—5663
Third Class														
1906-1911	573	51	134	21	69	8	14	3			33	16	1	923
1912-1916	1701	260	280	45	140	4	5	15	7	3	84	251	9	2804
1917-1921	1633	220	81	67	90	4	6	15	2		16	154	3	2321
1922-1926	3828	285	57	18	57	3	11	26	9		51	79	3	4427—1047
	13125	1727	1397	206	540	73	123	109	29	5	434	637	26	18440—18440

5315 students received their academic training outside of Saskatchewan

18   *Report of Department of Education, 1926*, p 52

XIII   REGULATING THE SUPPLY OF TEACHERS

In 1917 the Provincial Legislature passed three measures which
had an important bearing on the available supply of teachers for the
schools of the Province.

The "School Attendance Act" required the regular attendance at
school of all pupils over seven and under fourteen years of age, unless they had passed the grade eight examination before attaining
their fourteenth birthday The maximum age of compulsory attendance has since been raised to fifteen years Other amendments
to the School Act required all schools in the province to be in operation at least two hundred teaching days during each calendar year
The School Grants Act was also amended by which a special grant
of one dollar and fifty cents per day, afterwards increased to three
dollars per day, was provided for departments devoted exclusively to
pupils above grade seven in schools doing High School work These
measures greatly increased the number of pupils who wrote on the
public school leaving examinations, and who went on to take the
High School work, with a resulting increase in the number of candidates who wrote the examinations for teachers' certificates

Under the amended regulations which became effective in 1924,
third class certificates were valid only until December 31st of the
second year following the period of training After which time the
holder of such certificate might qualify for an Interim First or Second
Class certificate, according to his academic standing, by completing a
Normal School Course of training of eighteen weeks

The long-continued difficulty of securing and maintaining an
adequate supply of qualified teachers for the schools of the province
has now been overcome and the supply is really in excess of the
demand In 1926 only twenty provisional certificates were granted
Formerly the Department found it necessary to invite to the province, teachers from the British Isles and the other provinces of Canada, but owing to the rapid development of the province and the
consequent large number of school districts organized each year, it
was necessary for the Department to issue each year many provisional certificates From 1906 to 1916 inclusive, over 43 per cent of
the students attending the Normal School sessions received their
academic training outside the province From 1906 to 1926 inclusive
the Department issued 11,153 certificates to teachers trained outside
of the province, and during the same years 12,296 provisional certi-
cates were granted.

In 1926 the Third Class sessions of the Normal School were
abolished and the Department discontinued the practice of granting
standing to Third Class teachers from outside the province Since
then no Third Class certificates have been issued by the Department

The Normal School sessions were extended from thirty-three to thirty-eight weeks and the standard for a pass at the departmental examinations for a teacher's certificate was raised from 35% to 50% on each paper

In September 1926, so great was the number of students seeking admission to the Normal Schools, that the Department was unable to accommodate all who wished to enter, and it was necessary to continue holding local sessions of the Normal School at six different centres of the Province during the fall of that year

The increased number of students, due to the effect of the three Acts mentioned, notwithstanding the extension of the Normal School session to thirty-eight weeks, and the raising of the age of admission to eighteen years, made it necessary to open a new Normal School in the autumn of 1927

XIV SOME RECENT DEVELOPMENTS IN PROVINCIAL
CONTROL

At the Session of the Legislature held in 1928, a new departure in
education in Saskatchewan was instituted which will provide an
easier means of access to secondary education for the boys and girls
in the rural areas of the province and at the same time enable them
to remain on the farm Permissive legislation was enacted and assented to March 7, 1928, whereby winter high schools may be established in districts desiring them, which, owing to the seasonal
nature of agricultural pursuits on the prairies, will enable the boys and
girls to devote the summer half of the year to assisting with the
work on the farm while providing them the means of pursuing their
secondary education during the winter Coupled with this new idea,
is that of providing increased supervision for rural and village schools
which has been urgently demanded for some time by the Trustees'
Association

The legislation permits any three or more contiguous rural,
rural and village, or rural and town school districts to establish a
winter high school, provided that one of the school districts concerned is prepared to lease proper accommodation for the purpose
A winter high school board may lease grounds, buildings, etc , but
shall not have power to purchase school grounds, or power to purchase or erect school buildings or to incur expenditure other than
for the purpose of the current year [1]

The management or administration of a winter high school shall
be vested in a winter high school board composed of the several
chairmen of the school districts included at any time in the winter
high school districts, and the chairman of the school district in which
the winter high school is located, shall be the chairman of the winter
high school board

The school year for winter high schools shall be from the fifteenth of October to the thirtieth day of April The amount of
money required for the maintenance of the school shall be apportioned among the municipalities concerned in the same manner as
the taxes to be levied for ordinary school purposes [2] A rate of taxation will be levied over the whole area which together with the
grants will be sufficient to pay the Principal's salary together with
any other expenses incidental to the high school work

"The board may, in its discretion, charge every pupil or
the parent or lawful guardian of every pupil,

(a) a fee not exceeding ten dollars for the first term and fifteen

---

1 *Secondary Education Act, 1928*
2 *The Rural Municipalities Act*, s 302, p 103

dollars for the second term in any year, if the parent or lawful guardian is a resident ratepayer of the district,

(b) a fee of twenty dollars for the first term and thirty dollars for the second term if the parent or lawful guardian is not a resident ratepayer of the district Provided that the board may charge fees mentioned in clause (a) without charging those mentioned in clause (b) and vice versa "

The fees chargeable under clause (b) shall not apply if the rural municipality, village or town, under an agreement with the board by virtue of the power conferred by the respective Municipal Acts pays to the board in respect of pupils resident within the municipality, the fees charged under clause (b)

The Principal will be the employee of the whole area and as such will be the supervisor not only of the school in which the high school work is being carried on, but as well of all the schools in the winter school area He will commence his duties with the opening of the schools after the summer vacation by organizing and unifying the work in all the schools of the area concerned before the 15th of October when he will take charge of the winter high school work After his pupils have written their examinations on or about April 15th, he will again assume his duties as supervisor of the elementary schools in the area The Principal will be a full time employee working throughout the scholastic year in the interests of the entire district

The money required for the maintenance of a winter high school shall be raised by each of the interested municipalities in accordance with the following terms of the Act

"(1) On or before the first day of February in each year, or in the case of a district established subsequently to the first day of February, as soon thereafter as possible, the board of trustees of a winter high school district shall transmit to the treasurer of each municipality in which the district is wholly or partly situated a certified copy of a resolution of the board showing the share of the amount required for the maintenance of the school payable by such municipality, and the council shall levy within the district or portion of the district, as the case may be, such rates as shall be sufficient to provide that share

"(2) The amount required for maintenance of the school shall be apportioned among the municipalities in the same manner as the taxes to be levied for ordinary school purposes

"(3) The rate required to raise the said share shall be added by the council to the school rates of the district or portion of the district concerned and collected therewith

"(4) The council shall pay to the winter high school board its share of the district's requisition in equal instalments on the twenty-eighth day of February, the thirtieth day of April, the thirty-first day of October and the thirty-first day of December "

It is felt that this provision for winter high schools will give all the advantages of the small district area in maintaining local interest in school administration together with the benefits of the larger unit, without in any way interfering with the working out of the present school law, besides it has the additional strong feature that a boy can be of assistance on the farm during the busy months of the year and at the same time secure his matriculation standing It is hoped by this means to give the rural pupils the full advantage of a secondary education without necessarily divorcing them from agricultural pursuits

---

THE OUTPOST CORRESPONDENCE SCHOOL

In February 1925, the Department of Education alive to the lack of educational facilities for the children of families living outside of regularly organized school districts, and in the frontier settlements of Saskatchewan, established what is known as "The Outpost Correspondence School" to provide such children with very essential help in covering the course of studies in the eight grades of the public school

The "School" is under the management of an experienced teacher, individual lesson-sheets containing directions or material for study are mailed to the pupils, who are required to perform the work outlined and to submit at least a part of the work done for inspection and correction There is no charge for tuition, and copies of the 'Canadian Readers" in use in Saskatchewan are supplied free by the Department to the pupils doing work in Grades I to VI inclusive Each family is also supplied with a copy of the "Programme of Study" and other helpful pamphlets from the Departments of Education, Agriculture, and Public Health The Federal Government has also been requisitioned for pamphlets dealing with bird-protection, bee-keeping, sanitation, etc [1]

The pupils enrolled in the "School" live chiefly in the northern and south-western parts of the province Two of the children live on the north bank of the Churchill River which is about three hundred and fifty miles north of Regina, others are as far as twenty-five miles from the nearest school

The "School" opened with an enrolment of seven pupils in February 1925, and this number steadily increased as the work undertaken by the school became known One hundred pupils were enrolled during 1925 At the end of 1926 the total enrolment was 190 pupils—100 boys and 90 girls, while in 1927 the enrolment was 153 boys and 133 girls [2]

Many requests for tutorial assistance come from homes in organized school districts during the winter season when the local school is closed or too far distant for the younger children to attend Such help can not be given as the "School" was established only for children living in rural districts who cannot secure an

---

1   *Report of Department of Education, 1926*, p 94

2   *Annual Report Department of Education, 1927*, p 110

82

education in any other way   Exceptions are made in the cases of,

> (a) children who are physically unable to attend their local rural school,
>
> (b) children living in organized school districts situated in "Soldier Settlements" in which the school houses have not yet been erected [3]

The enrolment by grades during the year 1927 was as follows

Grades	I	II	III	IV	V	VI	VII	VIII	Total
Pupils	132	42	39	20	23	12	11	9	286

That this very worthy departure in education on the part of the Department of Education is greatly appreciated by the pupils of the "School", and their parents, is evidenced by the many letters of thanks and commendation received from them by the teacher-in-charge   The benefits of the "School", (and who can measure them,) in opening the door of opportunity to those children, cannot help but be far-reaching and will amply repay the province for the assistance it is extending to them

—————————

ACT RESPECTING ASSISTANCE FOR SOLDIERS' DEPENDENT
CHILDREN

The Education of Soldiers' Dependent Children Act—General provision was made at the session of the Legislative Assembly in February 1920 for the education of the children of deceased or disabled soldiers who had fought in the "Great War" and who were resident in Saskatchewan at the time of their enlistment or draft, and in respect of whom also a pension is being paid

Assistance is given to such when they have passed the Grade VIII examination or its equivalent and may be continued for a period of three years or until the child has obtained Junior Matriculation or Grade XI standing   The limit of assistance is two hundred and forty dollars for the scholastic year of ten months   The administration of this Act is placed in the hands of a commission consisting of the Deputy Minister of Education as chairman, a person nominated annually by the Minister of Education, and a person nominated annually by the executive committee of the Saskatchewan Command of the Great War Veterans' Association   The Act came into force May 1st, 1920   This commission has full power and authority and exclusive jurisdiction to deal with all matters pertaining to the assistance to be given, subject to the provisions of the Act

3   *Report of Department of Education, 1926*, p 15

Before an applicant may be granted assistance, he must submit
to the Commission

(a) a certificate of good character,

(b) a certificate or other satisfactory evidence of the date of
birth,

(c) a certificate from a duly qualified medical practitioner that
he is physically fit to carry forward a course of studies,

(d) proof that pension allowance has been payable [1]

The applicant must secure from the Commission the approval of
the educational institution which he desires to attend, and must
make at least eighty per cent of the possible attendance in each
month, except for reasons satisfactory to the Commission

The number of students receiving the allowance has steadily
increased from 3 in 1920 to 244 in 1927   The amount expended in
grants in 1927 was $38 907 65 [2]

In the case of one child in a family receiving assistance, the
grant is twenty-four dollars per month, for the second child the grant
is eighteen dollars per month, and for the third or other children it
is twelve dollars per month

The majority of the children who have benefited under the Act
since it came into force are the children of men whose lives were lost
overseas   These are living in the cities of the province and are in
attendance at the city collegiate institutes where many of them are
enrolled in the "Commercial Course"

The following statement gives the percentage of disability of the
soldiers whose applications for assistance were successful during the
year, and the number of children of deceased soldiers whose guardians
applied for assistance and were granted the same [3]

Children of deceased soldiers	32
Children of soldiers with a disability over 50%	9
Children of soldiers with a disability over 25% and under 50%	9
Children of soldiers with a disability of 25% and under	24
	74

EDUCATIONAL DEVELOPMENT

As an index of the growth of education in the province since the
first Board of Education was organized in 1885, the following facts
taken from a recent report of the Department of Education are il-
luminating   In 1927 there were 211,599 children attending the elementary schools of the province, and 6,961 students in high schools
organized under the Secondary Education Act   There was spent by
the school boards approximately $16 000 000 00, including the amount

1   *Revised Statutes of Saskatchewan, 1920,* c 116, and *Report of Department
of Education, 1921,* p 107
2   *Report of Department of Education, 1927,* p 121
3   *Ibid , 1926,* p 117

borrowed and paid on notes. The estimated value of the rural elementary school buildings was $12,723,663 39 and of the village' town and city school buildings was $14 198,676 35, a total of $26,-922,339 74, against which there is a debenture indebtedness of $11,797 472 91 of which $8,562,398 50 is in the villages, towns and cities   To the rural schools the provincial government paid in grants, $1,270,534 90 and to the village, town and city schools $870,754 93, while the grants to high schools and collegiate institutes during the same year were $199,245 74   During 1927 thirty-six per cent of all money spent and distributed by the government from revenue account was used for the promotion of education [5]

With reference to the financial statement of Table XV which shows the receipts, expenditures etc , for all elementary schools for certain years, it is advisable to tabulate in greater detail the sources of income and also the items of expenditure for one of those years, e g , 1927

The chief sources of revenue were [6]

Proceeds from taxes	$10,415,004 73
Fees received	124,006 82
Government grants	2,141,289 83
Proceeds of debentures	1,300,862 09
Borrowed by note	1,663 168 63
Other sources	346,639 82

The principal expenditures were

Teachers' salaries	$ 7,184,460 04
Grounds and buildings	2,116,040 64
Furniture and equipment	305,507 13
Libraries	54,364 62
Van-drivers' wages	211,632 65
Conveyance equipment	9,558 03
Fees paid	31 022 07
Paid on debentures	1,459,628 62
Paid on notes	1,815,173 28
Other expenditures	2,677,035 42

For the same year the total receipts for secondary schools, exclusive of money borrowed by notes or debentures which amounted to $477,018 63, were $760,775 81   Of this sum $199,245 74 was received from legislative grants and $73,239 12 from fees [7]

The expenditures for secondary schools in 1927, not including money paid on notes or debentures which amounted to $345,118 93, were $843,179 35   The amount expended in payment of the salaries of the 225 teachers employed in the high schools and collegiate institutes was $508,772 34, an amount almost equivalent to the salaries paid—$520,646 64—to the teachers in all the school districts of the North-West Territories[8] in 1904, the year preceding that in which Saskatchewan became a province

---

5   *Report of Department of Education, 1927,* p 13, 14
6   *Ibid , 1927,* p 32
7   *Ibid , 1927,* p 41, 44
8   *Ibid , 1904-1905,* p. 17

TABLE XV   GROWTH OF EDUCATIONAL FACILITIES IN SASKATCHEWAN
ELEMENTARY SCHOOLS.

| | Districts having Schools in operation | Departments in Operation | Total Enrolment of Pupils | | Districts (at end of year) | | | Receipts of all Schools | Expenditures of all Schools | Debenture Indebtedness | Government Grants |
			Rural Schools	Town Schools	Public School	Roman Catholic Separate School	Protestant Separate School				
1906	873	1017	23,125	8,150	933	7	2	$ 1,465,361 80	$ 1,448,914 69	$ 941,833 68	$ 174,218 34
1911	2110	2480	42,548	29,579	2544	14	2	4,029,781 57	3,989,036 28	2 668,596 13	533,437 82
1916	3608	4279	74,387	51,203	3859	16	3	9,312,694 32	9,211,389 76	6,068,423 77	969,700 14
1921	4268	5591	102,478	75,490	4459	17	4	14,988,691 45	15,174,524 36	10,982,244 00	1,346,458 85
1926	4506	6220	122,973	82,989	4693	22	6	14,956,014 11	14,789,956 18	10,802,891 69	2,033,761 45
1927	4518	6377	126,483	85,116	4745	23	8	15,990,971 92	15,917,668 47	11,797,472 91	2,141,289 83

BIBLIOGRAPHY

———— -

This bibliography contains the references which have been especially helpful in preparing this thesis

1   *Statutes- of Canada, 1871*, c 16, p 84, *1875*, c 49, p 261, *1888*, c 19, p 110

2   *Journals of the Council of the North West Territories, 1877*, p 5, 10, 24, *1878*, p 39, 40, *1883*, p 6, 7, 33, *1884*, p 7, 13, 80, 81, 97, *1885*, p 4, 7, 39

3   *Ordinances of the North West Territories, 1885*, No 3, s.1, p 533, *1887*, No 2, s 1, 10, p.3, *1888*, c 59, s 37-41, p 437, *1896*, No 2, s 12, 96, 106, p 9, *1901*, c 29, s 3, 8, 10, 11, 107-130, p 200

4   *Journals of the Legislative Assembly of the North West Territories, 1890*, p 21, 40, *1893*, p 109

5   Black, Norman F , *History of Saskatchewan*, Saskatchewan Historical Co , Regina, p 123, 196, 198

6   Oliver, E H , *The Canadian North West*, Publications of Canadian Archives, No 9, p 1001, 1034, 1035

7   Clement, Hon W H P , *The Canadian Constitution*, The Carswell Co , Toronto, c 38, p 777

8   *Reports of the Board of Education, North West Territories, 1886-1887*, p 11, 15, 18, 27, 51, *1887-1888*, p 10, *1888-1889*, p 8, *1889-1890*, p 7, *1890-1891*, p 21

9   *Reports of the Council of Public Instruction, N W T , 1896*, p 8, 16, 17

10   *Reports of the Department of Education, N W T , 1902*, App D, *1903*, p 12, *1904-1905*, p 17, 27, 32-35

11   *Reports of the Department of Education, Saskatchewan, 1906*, p 7, *1908*, p 7, 10, 11, 20, 21, *1913*, p 9, 14, 15, *1914*, p 33, *1915*, p 23, 24, *1916*, p 9, 18, *1919*, p 58, 94, 98, *1921*, p 11, 45, 107, *1924*, p 52, 52a, *1926*, p. 13, 15, 52, 67, 94, 117; *1927*, p 13, 14, 32, 37, 39, 41, 44, 86, 88, 110, 121

12   *Statutes of Saskatchewan, 1907,* c 25, s 10, 11, 37, 38, 49-51,
61, 62, *1908,* c 7, s 3, *1912-1913,* c 30, s 4, 167a, *1920,* c 23,
s 3, 21-23, c 109-113, p 1852, c 116, p 1193, *1927,* c 34, s 49,
1928, c 48, s 14, 18

13   *Acts of the Legislature of Saskatchewan,* King's Printer, Regina,
The School Assessment Act, 1926, s 34, 35, 44-51
The Assessment Commission Act, 1922, s 14
The City Act, 1926, s 13, 14, 329-354, 432-437
The Town Act, 1927, s 14, 15, 41, 79, 80, 462a, 574
The Village Act, 1928, s 8, 29, 35, 243, 247, 305 309
The Act Respecting Rural Municipalities, 1928, s 21, 173,
221, 224-250, 301, 302, 312-315
The School Grants Act, 1913, 1920, 1928
The Secondary Education Act, 1907, c 25, *1920,* c 109, *1924,*
c 23, *1928,* c 47

14   *Census of Saskatchewan, 1926,* Dominion Bureau of Statistics, p 80, 81, 83, 178

15   *Annual Survey of Education in Canada, 1927,* Dominion
Bureau of Statistics, p xiv, xxiii, 23, 29, 74, 77

16   Foght, Harold W., *A Survey of Education in Saskatchewan,*
King's Printer, Regina, *1918,* c 2, 3, 15